ISBN: 0-692-65776-2
ISBN-13: 978-0-692-65776-8

Library of Congress Control Number: 2016903865
Moor Publishing House
Philadelphia, Pennsylvania USA
i.did.fulfill@gmail.com

Published 2016

Editors:
Torianna Guy
Lawrence Pitilli

Cover Design
Graffiti Communications
www.graffitidesigns.us

'Daddy, Don't Touch Me There.'

One woman's story of survival

By: Monique Doran

Preface

-This book is for those of us who have been molested and understand it.

-This book is also for those who haven't been molested; those who could never truly understand, but could help someone heal.

- This book is to educate people, because so many have the power to see the signs, which could help even one child, woman, boy or girl from ever having the horrid memory of molestation.

-Most of this book is for all the SURVIVORS.

Acknowledgement

To my spirit, my very will to live, I first give thanks, for had that been broken I would have been but another victim of the rape culture. To my one and only baby girl Ajhanae', thank you for choosing a vessel that needed mending. For being patient with me, loving me to wholeness, not once have you ever given up on your mommy.

Tori, you remain a mystery still, why you came is no longer unknown, why you chose to become a permanent place of healing and growth in my life, is beyond me, but for it all I thank you.

To Mrs. Wilson from Roxborough H.S and Ms. Martin from Mona H.S. Kingston Jamaica, who both taught me where humility and believing in one's self can take them, I am eternally thankful.

To Tasha Williams, for all the things you have done, the times you have been there too numerous to list here, I thank you.

To my cousin Trudy-Ann Carruthers who always took me in off the streets, you continue to be a blessing. To all my family and friends that loved me even when most thought I was crazy and worthless, thank you.

A special thank you to Stephen Crawford and Khamour Brown, two very special men, who showed me how very possible it was to value men of honor, restoring my trust once more, giving me love in its most honest and purest form

My professor Lawrence Pitilli who met a young misguided girl with a Jamaican accent, but helped in opening my eyes to who I could be, promising to edit my book if ever I was so bold, and staying true to your word so many years later, I sincerely thank you.

To my parents I say thank you, for teaching me the greatest lesson, the lesson of true forgiveness. You taught me that what was meant for bad can indeed be used for good. Most of all you showed me that as long as I can find the strength to smile, I'll be just fine.

To every person that ever called me a menace to society without giving me a fair shot, I thank you, because you reminded me how important it was to write this piece, to give hope to the next Monique you may bump into on the way.

Saving the most precious for last, to my fellow survivors, for taking the time to pick up these few words, I thank you. I know the courage it took to give hope one last try. I bless these words infinitely, knowing when you read them, they will become a tool to assist you in taking your power back, and becoming the beacon you were meant to be. Take comfort in knowing that each time you smile, you rob your wrongdoers of your power they intended to hold forever. Remember that each smile is a frown they wished, but you turned it upside down.

1.

You never expect your first thoughts of sexuality to be triggered by your own father, but such is the tale I have to tell. When I was 11 years old many things in my life began to change. High school commenced, and new body parts grew, and with that cross over from childhood came many new elements of life a child could hardly prepare themselves for.

Prior to this time period, my life was a simple but very happy one. I grew up in what was considered a normal home, well at least to us, in Kingston Jamaica. A mother, father, and my sister, who is my junior by almost three years, but financial hardships had forced my mother to leave the island, just like so many other parents had to before her. At that age, when you find yourself living in a 5 bedroom home, with a yard big enough to house two more like it, be blessed to have hired help, while you hear of others who barely had food to eat, it proves quite hard to understand what financial hardship was. It took a few years, and some growing up to truly understand the behind the scenes of it all. In her leaving it meant that I was in the sole custody of my father, naturally. He was at the time a sergeant in the Jamaican Constabulary Force, and I was proud of that. It almost felt like an accomplishment to me as a child. Some persons when told of my father's occupation, almost seemed to offer a sense of reverence, which served to provide a sort of code of protection while at school, as no one dared to "trouble policeman pickney". He had an innocent smile that allowed everyone in his presence to feel safe. And I being a child was no different. In fact I was consumed by his charm, as he always played the daddy dearest role better than anyone I knew at the time. He spoilt us, gave us most things our hearts desired, always made play time for us, weekend outings to beaches all over the island, so naturally he won father of the year with us every year.

He was an equally stern man, demanding only the best from us in matters of school and behavior, and made no joke about putting fire to my tail if needs be. After my 12th birthday, something changed in him. I suppose paying close attention now one could say it perhaps began before then, but only then did they become so blatantly clear, once I was considered no more a child.

Why was his hand on my thighs, I thought to myself. This was certainly strange. We were watching TV together as we always did in the evening's right before the nightly news came on. Today was different though. Today my father decided his open palm would be rested on my upper thigh, leaving me feeling strange, and odd.

This is my father, it must be just some mistake, perhaps he hadn't realized. The weird feeling gave me my first panic attack of many to come. I got up to use the bathroom, as a tactic to change my sitting place. I returned to living room, choosing a seat across from him, and my father gave me a look I had never seen in his eyes before. Something changed. I could feel it, but understanding and coming to terms with what that change was, would prove to be the hardest. A few days past and no more incidents took place, I shrugged off the situation, thinking maybe it's all the new changes I was going through. Maybe I was overthinking everything.

Just as I had the thought and let my mind relax, he came home that evening, and right on my lips landed an unusual kiss. Eww I remember thinking to myself and a few what the fucks. I slammed my hands into my lips, wiping them so hard; trying my best to undo what had just been done. With lips as dry as the desert sands, eyebrows meeting, and anger on my breath I asked, what are you doing? He paused for a moment, then turned to face me and said, "I was just saying good evening". He walked away carelessly as if it was just another day, business as usual, while I just stood there dumbfounded, still and numb.

This is the part where many would say, that's not such a bad thing, dads kiss their daughters all the time. But this was different. He was being different, and his wet lips staying on my face 30 seconds too long said it all. The thing is though, I wasn't overthinking it, things were definitely changing and at a very rapid pace. What was once lap time became come sit on daddy's lap, the tone being the culprit and the context its partner in crime. If you could hear it as I still do today, you would cringe at the very thought of it. A hug became an embrace lasting too long, now ending with his penis perfectly positioned between my thighs, but I was innocent and my imagination had not fully matured to what he insinuated, my thoughts weren't even in the same postal code as his actions. My logical brain knew that this feeling, these actions, were wrong, to be reported, and by all means rejected. But I was 12 and my emotional brain took hold, and logic made no sense. How could it be correct after all? This new feeling of immorality had to be wrong. This was my father, and he wouldn't bring me harm? He saved people, helped them, and arrested the bad guys, how could he himself become just that? So I dismissed it as nothing, telling myself, I had to be wrong, that my hormones changing up had to be playing a role in all of this. The more I tried though to prove my father's innocence, the worst things became.

The hugs and kisses became slaps on my thighs and grabs on my ass. My breast became target practice for his eyes, and the authority I was under, seemed lifted just a bit. Emotions and logic went right through the door now, leaving me in a state of anger and confusion. I became paranoid about myself and mind, wondering why no one else noticed or if perhaps my mind was just playing tricks on me. One Saturday while raking the yard we happened to be alone under the huge Bombay mango tree that stood in the front. A tree under which I had many beautiful memories, which made it just that much harder to ask the question I was about to ask. Looking up at my father, staring in his squinted brown eyes, as still as I could be, and in some sense, feeling like my heart had stopped, hoping that his answer, the answer I'd hoped to hear, would hit the restart button. I asked shyly, afraid of the outcome, "why you start to touch me on my thighs, why the kissing and grabbing of my butt?" He gave me the coldest stare one could ever imagine, and suddenly I knew that button was going to be left untouched, and a sort of death would begin. He shouted sternly, but in a soft roar "how dare you, you little rass, you are out of order". "You think me and you a size?" Immediately a sudden rush of fear ran up my spine, for I knew I was in the right, and this was all just plain wrong, I didn't need age or maturity to tell me that.

After what seemed like an eternity of silence, followed by a how fucking dare you stare, his voice filled the air with the words to confirm, "I am your father how dare you?" "I am being a father to you, showing you love and affection, and you come with you dirty mind thinking me and you are the same size and company?" "Don't ever let me hear you ask me any foolishness like that again. I am your father, and I am here to show you love".

Temporary dismissal of what I believed to be true was the action in play. I reasoned to myself, rationalized, looking at it from every angle, every point of view. My father was a good man, a silent man, with the sweetest most honest smile, he was the best father, and he would never violate his parental duties like that. Hell no! I convinced myself I was tripping, even if it was only a temporary thought.

2

Summer break was here, which meant the end of my freshman year at Mona High School. It also meant that we'd be headed off to the states for about a month or so to visit my mother. Ever since I was 10 years old and got my American visa, leaving the island was something we looked forward to every year. Seeing my mother was ok I suppose. She was never the most relatable person, and our relationship was never a close or bonding one, but the trips to Dorney Park, Six flags, and just enjoying the likes of "merica" made it all worth it at that age.

This trip felt different though, this trip the question of telling my mother what was going on or if there was even something going on weighed heavily on my mind. Every day I hoped and prayed things would go back as they once were. If my father could just go back to being the nice policeman everyone respected and loved including me, but it only go worst. He became more physical with me, more disgusting, and very vile. The kiss on the lips became his tongue in my mouth. The first time, I was sitting in the big blue based floral printed settee facing the TV, as I did any other day, when suddenly my head titled backwards, followed by his big pink wet tongue entering my mouth. In a quick leaping motion I thrusted my arms backwards, almost coming up with all my might, but I held it, for my brain had quickly calculated that it would not have ended in my favor. The slaps on my behind became long grabs, and the accidental bumping into my tender, developing breasts on purpose, but by accident, if you see what I mean, was all beginning to wear thin on my nerves.

He was my hero though, so I had to be wrong about all this, and so I decided to give him one last chance. I thought to myself, he doesn't mean anything by all this; it's just that he doesn't know that it's uncomfortable. Maybe he was just giving me love as he had said before.

Finding the most innocent voice I could, and as humbly as I could, I approached him one more time, in hopes of restoring what once was, I said, "daddy when you put your tongue down my throat and do the other things to me, I don't like it. It makes me feel so uncomfortable and strange; could you please stop, please?" This little creep had the nerve to open his mouth to form the words that I was out of place again. Me! I'm the one that's out of place? I stood there once again, motionless, only this time I knew for sure my heart had definitely stopped beating. I was brought back to reality by the high pitched voice yelling at me screaming so angrily, I seriously thought for a second I was in the wrong. "I put a roof over your head, I make sure you eat and get to school, take care of you, and you want to question my authority? So that's what you want to go and tell your mother, that me doing things to make you feel strange?" He let me know that he no longer cared what happened to me, that I should no longer expect affection from him. The conversation in itself felt so weird and wrong, but that was a price I was willing to pay.

At last we landed in Philadelphia, and a sense of peace filled my soul, still my heart remained heavy, for I knew my father's behavior had to be addressed, but what's word without some sort of backing? What good did it do me to speak on something of which I had no proof? I thought of all the nosey neighbors who managed to always know when I was up to no good, but could not be called on in support of my testimony, they all saw that I was rude but no one ever really tried to find out what the underlying cause was. Parading on as normally as I possibly could, was all I focused on that summer, thinking of what hell would break loose once I returned home. There was going to be a full-fledged war in that house, and I could feel it in my bones. I just couldn't shake the feeling; the only thing I could focus on was being the last person standing when the dust settled.

Our return home was nothing like the other times before. Sure it brought with it a new school year as did all the others, and another birthday as all others, but all the other norms and ways of life I was accustomed to, crumbled, and a life altering change stirred. My 12th birthday gave me the gift of a menstrual cycle, and if you're closely following the story then you know inevitably that my father's lust for me only increased when this happened.

While washing the dishes one day, lost in thought, staring through the passage that connected both sides of the house, feeling empty, resenting the changes that had been taking place, I heard a whisper in my ear "you like what I did to you last night?", instantly I dropped the tea cup I'd been washing, and my mouth followed suit as it hit the floor in disbelief. I had not been told what exactly happened last night, but every part of my being knew and felt the words, actions, and thoughts to follow would be the beginning of the end, that all hell was about to break loose. I knitted my eyebrows so tightly that I seemed to be looking through one eye, and before I could ask for a repetition of that statement, I heard my father say "when I came home from work last night I came into your room, shifted your panty and played with you. You smiled as you slept, because I know you loved it". That was it! The last domino had just been tipped over, and the whole thing was about to come down. See to this day, sleep is my surrender zone, once I'm out, that's it. I wondered how far he'd really gone, but truth proved to be a much harder medicine to swallow.

Armed with the truth I made it my mission to protect me and my little sister at all costs. Everything changed so fast. The one confession became a regular thing as every evening when he came home from work he would tell me how he came into my room and pleasured me, by slipping his fingers inside of me.

When I wasn't going through that BS I was dealing with the groping or his threats. His worst arsenal were the promises, as each time I said I was going to tell my mother, he promised to get help. Naturally he had already played father dearest, winning our affection, leaving me hopeful each time, believing there was hope, that he would change, but things only worsened. Reaching the peak of my tolerance, I told him I'd had enough and was definitely going to report him; his reply was the most threatening look I'd ever seen in the eyes of a man. He let out a most loud sarcastic laugh, and then jeeringly said "Who are you going to tell? I am the authority," reminding me that he was the law, he also made sure I knew that he wouldn't hesitate at any moment to kill me, and everyone in the house, leave the island, then off him and my mom. That was a scary thought as a 12 year old, knowing that if you spoke up for yourself, you could end all those lives. Things would never be the same but this I never saw coming, this animal was preparing me to be his woman. He had strength, authority, and power in his favor, and would need them all in accomplishing such a grotesque feat. He became unknown to me; he became a monster that I didn't know. He became an enemy, as the father I once knew was dead, or lost somewhere.

Jennifer the hired help became the closest person I had where a mother was concerned. She did the best she could to understand my behavior and outbursts, why I began to change, but she was in line with many other teachers, deans and even the principal. I'd been known to dish out some good ole ass whooping if ever I felt violated, but now, I was like a trained fighting dog, freed from her leash. I fought for no reason, and every reason. I didn't smile anymore and lost my silliness, became anti-social and silent. It was as if the sun inside had died. But all the grownups around me could see was my bad behavior; they never thought to ask why. I mean I agree picking up a desk and throwing it towards a student, simply because there's no other way to vent can never be justifiable, but there is always an underlying issue.

Sadly all that acting out was me simply wanting just that, someone, anyone, to ask that simple question, why? They didn't ask, and I simply wasn't strong enough all by myself to say something. But maybe, if someone were to start asking questions, maybe I'd start to talk and oops, everything would surely come pouring out. No questions came though; they saw only what they wanted to see.

Jennifer's daughter Julia would often come to spend the weekends at the house with us, not only did she provide good company, but also temporary protection.

See I would be on her like glue, which gave my father less opportunities to keep up his dirty deeds. This particular weekend, Julia's baby father and her had a really nasty fight, meaning she would be spending an entire week with us.

It was a breath of fresh air for me. I went outside, played like a normal kid, and pretended with all the other children as if all was well within the wall of the Doran kingdom. But this was short lived, as by the middle of his time being interrupted, he erupted.

Lounging about in the kitchen one afternoon after having a few colas, and sharing a few laughs, a sudden silence fell on Julia's face. When my brain caught up to reality, my father's hand had found its way to my rear end, Julia and I made eye contact, and it was as if my soul took a deep breath and then sighed. At long fucking last I thought to myself, someone else finally knew what was happening, and they got it from the culprit himself.

For just a second I allowed myself to feel hope, that she would surely tell her mom what was going on, but that hope died the second he looked in my eyes and said sorry. Just arrogantly smirked and said sorry. How do you apologize for violating my body in in that manner, for even having the thought to begin with? Surely Julia wouldn't buy into that? My disbelief knocked me to another realm, by the time I came back to reality, I was lifting the fork in my hand, ripping the skin on my father's arm. I stood there, unapologetic, awaiting the wrath I was sure he would lay on me, but nothing happened, he just walked away, looking to his arm, wiping the bright crimson, seeping from his wound.

Unfortunately the first and most taught and respected rule in my culture, of minding one's business when you "go to people yard" applied to my case in her eyes, and with that Julia saw nothing and said nothing to her mother, against all that I'd wished for. Nothing was the same after that moment. Whenever she came by the house she did her best to avoid my father, making every effort to keep her mouth and questions silent.

I came to the reality that no fairy god mother was coming to whisk me away. I'd have to rely on my will to survive, while hoping and praying that, this god I'd been sacrificing all my Sundays for, would show up and slay my Goliath. Until that happened I realized the threat was to take my innocence, I couldn't say for sure that he wouldn't over power me someday, but one thing I knew definitely, in the telling of the story of how my virginity was given, given would be the operative word, and my father's name was not going to be a part of it.

Sex I knew of, heard about from school friends, but sexuality and the actual experience of it, had never entered my thoughts on its own. I was a tomboy, sometimes shy, but still very present and innocent in every aspect of the word. But I realized I had to shed that if I intended on winning this war, and the first step was to find a most suitable prospect. If I was going to do this I was going to make it memorable and respectable.

3

Alrick stepped on the bus one Monday morning while I was on my way to school. His double blue shade J.C uniform was neatly ironed against his light bright skin, which complimented his eyes that couldn't seem to make up their minds what color they really wanted to be. As soon as I laid eyes on him I knew he would be my first attempt at taking away the prize my father so desperately sought.

Meanwhile at home things go from bad to just plain horrible. The worst part was Jennifer not picking up, blind to what was going on right in front of her very eyes, or seeing it but not helping me. Something about her daughter keeping her mouth shut must have amped my father's ego, because he was becoming more bold each day with his actions. He started coming into my room in the mornings while I got dressed for school, sitting on my bed, staring, taunting me with his eyes.

I felt disgusted, always wishing I could escape my body, if even only temporarily. When I was finished getting dressed, he would get up in a most creepy way, eyes focused on my body as he got close to me he would whisper in my ear, "you loved what I did to you last night" responding to the puzzled look on my face with a detailed story of how he used his fingers to play with my vagina the night before. As the vomit came to my throat each time, I took some solace in the fact that I was such a sound sleeper, making it just a bit easier to keep hope that maybe it was all a lie, thankful for not being alert to remember, because creating the memory would be the worst part.

After his little session one morning I'd gotten to the point of being tired of dealing with his crap. I didn't care what he would do to me; I had to tell someone what was going on. The threats no longer mattered, I'd rather to have been dead, than to keep living that way, so I sat on the edge of my bed, tore paper from my binder, and began writing.

In my note I mentioned that I was tired of the fuckery going on. My father wasn't my man, so I need not play the role of his woman, making it absolutely clear that if he did not leave me alone, I intended on running away. I folded the paper so tiny, as if my true intentions were to hide it, then carefully and strategically dropped it on a path I knew she'd take to wash clothes later that day, but making it all seem accidental. When I got home that day I could hear her screaming for me across the hall, the tone in her voice, the urgency, confirmed for me that my plan had worked and she had taken the bait. She motioned for me to close the door and then patted the bedside, signaling me to sit beside her.

In a soft, confused voice, she asked while bringing the piece of paper to view, "Monique, what is this? What is this you write about your father?" "You didn't even realize you drop it, eh?" Shaking my head at her profound ignorance, I let her know that it was my intent that she should have found that piece of paper, and that every word on it was true.

Both the paper and her mouth fell to the floor simultaneously, as she just sat there frozen, in disbelief over what she had just learned. My disbelief however, came when I realized she probably really honestly had no idea. She actually seriously in reality didn't know what was going on, or she was playing ignorant really well. After what felt like hours of unloading, giving her all the info she desired, I looked her square in the eyes, and asked how she could not see. "Didn't you notice the changes in his behavior towards me?" She hung her head, shaking in a no motion, not wanting to look up as her eyes got watery. Apart of me saw a woman who knew what was happening like everyone else but was too afraid of what their lack of silence may cause in regards to their lives. Everyone saw him as the law, and the law as I said, protects its own.

I gave her every disgusting detail of what had been happening to that point. The early morning sex-ed classes from him as he enjoyed watching me ready for school, how his attitude towards me changed, about the confrontation under the mango tree, how Julia saw what she saw, just everything.

I spoke until my words became teardrops, finishing the conversation in a language all of their own. It felt as though a massive burden had been lifted off my shoulders, as if my soul had been shallow breathing, then finally getting the chance to take a deep breath. She paced the room, bouncing off its green walls so hard; it was a wonder the paint remained intact. She mumbled, and muttered and bounced around some more, finally stopping next to me and with eyes filled with empathy said, "Monique, Mr. Doran is really a sick man", well let's talk beyond the obvious, I thought to myself, while I just sat there silently, allowing her to finish saying her piece. Just as she came to an end, she turned to me and asked why I never told my mom? I told her how he promised to get help, and I was praying that somehow it would be as it once was. She agreed that he needed help, because a man sick enough to desire his own child, is capable of just about anything.

This getting him help option was no longer working in my favor, so I asked her why we couldn't just report him to the proper authorities and send me to my mother, but she only confirmed what I thought her answer would be, what I'd heard so many times before, that he was the law, which gave him some advantage in the situation. She promised to talk to him when he came home that night, begging me to trust her to get him the help that he needed, that it would be alright in a short time. I knew her words wouldn't do anything to him, but I needed so badly to believe in her, and having no reason to doubt her I decided to just stay away from him as much as I possibly could, hope for the best, and avoid the worst.

Later that night, I could hear him sobbing in the room across the hall, while Jennifer questioned him, fooling her as much as he could that his tears were genuine, but not me, I wasn't moved. I'd seen those tears and heard that soft apologetic fake tone before. He pleaded for her to not take it to the authorities, promising to change, while admitting that he was indeed sick, and was in need of urgent help. He spoke of his love for his family, and his readiness to stop for his and our sake. But I saw right through his sack of shitting lies. His sobs were as empty as a tomb and the words were all recited, but believe it or not though she bought into it.

Looking back on it now, I suppose it's easier to forgive her and understand why. Charm is a gift my father used and abused, fortunately the puppy dog eyes had lost their effect on me, allowing me to see him for the monster he truly was, but the delay with which Jennifer handled things, left me to wonder if she was still a slave to his sly ways. Winning this battle all by myself, became so clear to me, I was a lone soldier.

Three things I was sure had to happen, I had to leave the island, I had to keep baby sis safe through all this, and at all costs ensure if even with my life that I did not end up telling a tale of how my father deflowered me.

Weighing the options before me, I rationalized what the next best move would be. The facts were, my mother was in America, she couldn't travel, Jamaica life wasn't easy, so didn't make sense to return, I knew for certain that's what she would have said, but if she knew what was happening I was sure she'd find a way to have us stay with her. The question now was how to go about telling her? I now also realized that he was more scared of being blasted by the authorities than I had previously thought, but it was still a slippery slope, and I'd heard enough in my short young years to fully understand the ropes. This mission was necessary and in order to win I remained humble, avoided him as much as possible, keep baby sis safe, study and sleep according to how his shift was set up, and tried to find some way of staying off the island for good the next time we left, keeping my innocence intact.

As if somehow he could hear my thoughts, or feel my vibrations, at the end of that week, enjoying my Saturday off from school, he approached me, and anger isn't capable of describing what he exuded. All the blood in his body rushed to his face, turning his once caramel skin crimson red. Just when I thought he was going to explode he blurted out, "I will kill you, kill everybody, in the house, take a flight to merica, kill your mother, and then turn the gun on myself". I went numb. He continued "if you ever say anything to your mom, or call my name to anyone else, you see what will happen." He told me that he was already dead and didn't care who he took with him, but he wasn't going to jail. A chill I could never explain went to my bones as I made eye contact with his lifeless, empty, dark eyes. My plans would not be easily shaken or deterred. Delayed? Maybe, but failing was never an option.

His threat only served to further concretize what I already felt in my heart to be true. Each day he became bolder, I realized more that I had to also keep steadfast with my plan as well. Alrick the young man I'd met on the bus became my closet friend, although I had a barrage of girlfriends from school, he somehow seemed like my only friend at the time, for he could save me in a way they could not. Here I was 12 years old, just a little time ago, all I wanted to do was hang with friends after school, but now being forced to jump a few years up the maturity ladder.

My new friend had no idea however of what was going on at home or that I chose him on purpose. We hung out every morning before school, as I would walk a couple miles down to Dunrobin to meet up in the mornings. I couldn't chance my father or anyone who knew my father spotting us. In the evenings we'd spend some time by his grandma's house before it was time to get home. On one of those occasions of going to granny's his supposed girlfriend approached me wanting to fight, accusing me of taking her honey. But if only she knew, yea I really liked him, but he was to be part of so much more than some emotional attachment. He stood up for me, and put her in her place, sent her away and ushered me into the house. He apologized while hugging me, so tight I melted, for these were the tight hugs of affection that I was lacking at home, true affection, not perversion. As I sat there on the bed my appreciation for his protection became overwhelming, I lunged at him and planted the first real, honest, pure and by choice kiss of my life. At that moment I knew what was going at home had to stop.

This was different; this was surrender by choice, the other surrender by force. He held my face in a sweet gentle way, looked in my eyes as if he was searching my troubled soul and even more sweetly said "Monique you're a sweet girl, take your time and grow. I don't want to hurt you". Inside my head a reality existed where I blurted out everything and the problem would be solved, then my father's voice, his threats, echoed in my ear, and suddenly that reality didn't seem so possible anymore, well at least for the moment. I tried again, and even though I had lied to him that I was 13, and he being 16 it wouldn't have been the worst situation, but he wouldn't budge because he thought me too young for such things. In that moment I had more love and respect for this young man than I did for my father. Sadly he was none the wiser that I was on a mission and if he couldn't help me complete it, then I had to overcome any emotions for him that would prevent my success.

At home things go from serious to urgent and they definitely showed no signs of changing for the better. One day while I was getting naked in the bathroom getting ready for my shower to head off to school, I heard the lock on the bathroom door opening, then all of a sudden it flung wide open with my father standing in the threshold, staring at my naked body, examining me with eyes that said I no longer have two fucks to give. As quickly as I could, I grabbed the towel from the floor and covered myself from the shame of his eyes. "Could you please get out and close the door behind you? I am naked and you shouldn't be in here". He looked me square and daringly in the eyes and said, "I have been giving you baths since you were a baby, so why all of a sudden I can't watch and make sure you bathe properly"? I told him I was no longer a baby, that I had lady parts now, and was more than capable of bathing myself.

That's what I said on the outside but on the inside I was screaming, because you are my father you sick son of a bitch. Silence fell in the room, that you could hear the sound of my tears hitting the tiles beneath my feet. I felt disgusting, and violated, I found the beast that stood in front of me repulsive, indeed a beast he must have been for he was no father mine.

No, my father died somewhere along the path, and I never got to say goodbye.

Finally after what seemed like forever, Jen showed up, hysterically asking what was going on, and what the loud noise was about. "Bitch please", I thought, as if you couldn't hear all that commotion. That coward (for only a coward would pick on a child) opened his filthy mouth to say that he had been giving me showers since I was a child, so why all of a sudden it became a problem?

I scanned the room to see what instrument would be most effective in ending this man's unnecessary life, while Jennifer just stood there, frozen, in disbelief I suppose.

Finally breaking her silence she raised her voice in an aggravated tone "Mr. Doran, she's a big girl now, having period now and all these things, she have parts you never used to wash, you can't do this." His hard, cold stare would have killed if it held the power to; walking away he reminded us that this was his house, he was in charge, swearing that killing us was no big thing to him.

My comfort in all of this was my little sister. Though only 3 years my junior, she was young enough to be totally naïve to the situation. She was my shield in some ways too I suppose.

At nights, I would wait to see which of the three beds in our room she'd pick for that night, and then cuddled up safely by her side. Even if she went on the tiny twin sized bed, I'd be right there beside her. Not only did it slow my father down, it helped me feel as if I was protecting her from him too.

I studied his schedule when he worked nights, trying as hard as I could manage to stay awake, if I managed, once I heard the door cracking open, I'd nudge my little sister, and with the sounds of her shuffle, he'd close the door, defeated. Little sister was so oblivious and innocent. She thought I was trying to annoy her as I usually did, so if she'd woken up to use the bathroom in the middle of the night, she'd often switch beds, and so as it goes, me being the deepest of sleepers would be so out of it, I'd realize in the morning. Some nights I got lucky, and he would only try once, or when he'd make his second attempt too soon and she'd still be beside me, safe for the time being.

One morning as he handed me my day's lunch money, he let me know how disappointed he was in me, I played the fool, asking what he meant by that, not really certain I'd really want the honest answer. Why are you sleeping with your sister at night? I furrowed my eyebrows, asking him why he was even in my room at nights. In a most strange and sadistic way, he smiled, reached for my face and said, "So I can check on you. You know, and make sure that you get your treatment". I could feel the warm vomit creeping up my throat, but I kept my cool, calmed my nerves and remembered the goal. At that moment I knew one thing for sure, he was beginning to care less and moving on with his plans more aggressively. Plans to take that from me which he hadn't given, nor been authorized by the laws of man or the universe to have. I was either going to kill him or force myself to have sex with someone else, quick, fast and in a hurry.

4

As destiny would have it one March morning in 99, I met what I considered at the time, my genie in a bottle. That morning, my favorite bus (you'd have to be Jamaican to understand) was late, as I fumbled and grumbled, looking at my watch repetitively, a young half bred Indian boy, with a rude boy swag emerged from the cracks in the wall that lead out of Watson drive, a hidden ghetto off White Hall Ave. That still voice inside spoke again, and I knew that he would be somehow important to my mission, and so as the next bus came and he ushered his sister onto the bus I stayed behind hoping to get his attention after.

As if I was being rewarded for following instructions, he turned to me with such a kind smile and asked why I hadn't gotten on the bus, I told him exactly as I heard it, he blushed, told me his name, and after a small chit chat waiting for the next bus, we made plans to meet up that afternoon.

That evening as he walked me home we talked about everything, stopping by people's gates, unbothered by my restriction on time, enjoying the others company. He was from the side of town I was often warned about. He was a "shotta" or "bad man", protected his turf and worked for the area leader. But he wasn't anything close to fitting the description I'd been given about people from his world. I was sure he'd done some things unworthy to be spoken of but he was so gentle and protective of his sister, and even with me a stranger, he was simply a product of what he saw. Such a gentleman he was, never even once bringing up the word sex.

I felt a sort of admiration for him, because he was so much younger than my father but more of a man. Our meet ups became an everyday thing and pretty soon I felt enough trust to chill with him at his home a few times. I thought him to be a great person to help me take what my father wanted, and possibly feeding two birds with one seed by having him eradicating my father all together. When I tried to send him hints though, he wouldn't take the reins, always reminding me that I was too young, too innocent. That he had a sister and he'd never want another man to know better and take advantage of her like that. I needed what I needed, but my respect for him made it effortless to understand him and his angle. I knew what my ultimate goal was so I let time do its work, while I strategized about protecting myself in the house.

Speaking of house it's as if my father sensed that some hairs where out of place, that something had changed. He became quite bold, as he upped the level of things. He would call me to the side of the house to have conversations about how beautiful and thick I was growing, and then another day about getting help, and yet another about his gun being emptied in my head. Everyone began noticing the changes and his new and odd behavior. How he began taking me on errands alone, instead of with me him and keta like it always was, changing the natural order of things, always isolating me. But yet again they only whispered no one ever cared to ask if all was well.

In the evenings he would have me open the gate for him, ensuring that if I intentionally opened his side first he'd call me back to his door to have a chat of did I remember last night. That part of it I could handle, I'd zone myself away to America and imagine better days. The physical part however, that took a whole different toll on me. When I couldn't avoid him, he'd sneak up on me, grab my vagina and breast quickly, always in a hurry, afraid of who may be just around a corner. For me though each round seemed to last forever. he intentionally slammed his tongue into my mouth each chance he got, taking pleasure on ending each session with story time about last night.

The end of the school year was approaching, I decided if somehow I managed to keep him off and out of me, and not kill him, make it to the states safely, my sister and I, then my troubles would be over. I had to fight and find some way; somehow to make it, I just had to hang on for a little while longer.

Speeding things up with Dwayne wasn't working as fast as I'd wished, but one particular afternoon in June something happened that altered the course more than I ever fathomed. I stopped by his house after school like I did most days before, only this day school was released early due to end of term exams. The rain had been falling heavily, since it was early and as far as I knew, no one knew my exam schedule, so I decided to stay at his house until the rain eased up a bit. This was the first we'd been all alone, and for so long, as his sister was out with friends.

We talked for hours asking each other every question we could summon to mind, about how the other half lived and felt. I found him so intriguing in that moment, and to know he could, but didn't try a thing my admiration grew and before I knew it my lips were planted firmly on his, replicating what my father had practiced on me so many times before, only this felt right, because again, it was my choice. After a few more minutes of kissing, he pulled me away, searched my eyes intensely, he said "Monique, you're a sweet girl, mi really rate you, but I can't do this to you. I have to allow you to grow, finish school, and make something of yourself". The only reply I could muster up came in the form of tears. If only he'd known that's all I truly wanted and yearned for, the chance to grow. I didn't really care about sex, I just wanted to day dream, play football, and have friends my age group, just be a kid.

By the time my brain caught up with reality, that's exactly what I was telling him. I broke down, fell into his arms and told him everything, from beginning to end. He joined me in the tears dance, as his eyes watered the more my story progressed. Giving me a big, safe and comfortable bear hug, he wiped my tears, and told me repeatedly how sorry he was for all that I'd been going through. Revealing my true plans for him made him blush for a moment, but the anger that he felt was much too strong. He assured me it wouldn't be necessary though, that if I could just somehow tough it out just a little while longer, he'd clean up this mess for me. All he asked was that I studied my father's schedule as detailed as possible, and have it ready when it was needed.

Between the tears and the talk, time went by faster than we'd realized, the rain had stopped and it was well over an hour past the time I should have been home on a normal day. For the first time in long while, I felt hope, or at least a glimpse of it, so I didn't care what happened to me when I got home. I'd gladly take the ass whooping I was sure I'd receive; my Romeo was planning my rescue mission. "Good evening" I smirked, as I waltzed through the doors at 4:30 pm.

"Where were you?" I told him I'd been up the street with a friend from school, by her mother's job. "Oh yea" he says, as he asks me this friends name and for me to take him to the house I had been at all day, as he had gotten wind that classes ended early. Inside I wished, prayed and hoped that she understood the language of the eyes, sensing the need for help in mine and that I would explain it all later. She managed to do the exact opposite though. We arrived at the house and I yelled through the grill on the veranda for Mrs. Channer, when she finally answered, my father asked if I had been there all evening or if she even knew me. She said she knew me, that I was her daughter's classmate and that I had been there before, and for a moment I held my breath hoping that maybe just maybe she did understand, I begged her with my eyes, please, please, just say yes I'd been there that day, but she just continued that I hadn't.

In her defense I suppose one can understand from her point of view how lying could have very well left me in more harm than good. She didn't know the situation.

He took me home and whooped my ass severely. He beat me as if he was a lover in a jealous rage, asking me, demanding repeatedly with each blow that I tell him where I had been all day, slapping the heavy leather belt all over my body. Numbness was the only sensation I felt after a while though. It didn't matter what he did, I didn't care, and that belt couldn't break me any more than he had already. Besides all that I, wasn't about to give up the one person that seemed to be looking out for my best interest and willing to help change the dynamics. When I'd had enough I thought quickly of a place called Duhaney Park that I'd only been to but once, but I'd remembered it was sort of a maze and easy to get lost in.

I led him on a wild goose chase, in and around all the streets, with not one clue as to where I was, hoping to tire him out enough he'd give up realizing all the houses looked the same. "Turn left, no right, I think it's this one, they all look the same" I said, "I can't remember."

Silence filled the car, and then a sudden slap connected with my scull, full force from his fist. "You think I am fucking stupid" he yelled while pounding me like a sack of flour. He stopped the car, put me out, and told me to make sure I'm right behind the van. Speeding up and slowing down, a few times even slamming the break for me to run into the back of the vehicle, punishing me for about 10 mins before letting me back inside. Halfway home he broke the silence demanding that I tell him where I was, making it clear that the information was coming out one way or another.

When we finally got home, I ran into my room, slammed the door and buried myself into the pillow, crying, hurt, angry and ashamed all at once. My sweet release was disturbed by a sudden burning feeling across my thighs, as if someone had set fire to them. By the time the second blow came I realized this sick twisted son of a bitch went outside and stripped the rubber from the windshield, and was now using it to lift the very skin from my muscles, like a scene from a slave movie. By the time he got to the fifth stroke I tapped out and agreed to tell him where I truly was. "I was up by a friend's house up in Watson Drive".

If this young man was as intelligent as I'd perceived him to be, then this could very well work. At the very worst I figured they could kill the fucker and be done with it. With blood still dripping from my thighs I hopped up in the truck and led him to my hopeful savior's home.

Ironically Dwayne was the one that came to the gate when I called out, the look he gave my father gave me the impression the day could have ended indeed in my favor, but he chilled and behaved like a smart soldier, playing the fool. He directed his focus to my thigh and the blood that was still dripping, immediately picking up the vibe. He told my father he wasn't sure if Dwayne was home, that he'd have to go check. My father's ignorance of

Dwayne's identity was a major benefit on our side. When Dwayne returned he informed my father that he left to attend a fete at Swallowfield primary, a nearby school up the street, and that's where he probably could be found.

That night ended with me beaten and lashed, shouting from neighbors now involved, but not really knowing the story behind the story, and Jennifer inside yelling about everything that was going on. I was ordered to change my clothes because we were going to the rape unit office.

Rape unit, I thought to myself as I slipped on a long yellow skirt, who the hell got raped? Ironically that night as we drove and silence filled the car, staring out the window I saw Dwayne and his brother walking right into the fete. Our eyes made four, time stopped, and in that second we were the only ones that existed. We shared a second, just a moment, but I could hear him tell me it would be ok, that he understood. That made my aching body feel so much better as I relaxed in the comfort he knew I didn't just snitch him out.

My whole body ached, from head to toe, I felt as if I'd been fighting all day, and got my ass served to me. Didn't bother me much though, because there was silence, still, crickets chirping drop a pin dead silence, for just a moment, just the thought of losing his prize infuriated him so much, he couldn't even speak. Further conformation my plan was necessary. "Where are we going?" I asked him, but it opened a whole other can of worms I wasn't prepared for. "Wait till your mom finds out about this. How could you? I gave you everything you need." It was in that moment, I truly understood just how very sick and dangerous my father was. As we drove into the parking lot, I saw a huge black and white sign that read, Rape and Juvenile Unit. As he parked the car, and I thought how my redemption was here, I glanced over towards him and saw something shiny on his thigh. It took me a few blinks of the eye to realize that I was in fact seeing a gun, small, but still very real, with a revolver, and his trigger finger looking for a reason. I looked into his eyes with pity and disgust. I searched his eyes trying to find the kindness I once knew, but it was replaced by a dark, cold emptiness. In an equally cold tone he said, "go in there, I called already they are expecting you, tell them your name. They will inspect you". "Inspect me for what daddy?" I asked. He told me they were going to see what I had done and how badly damaged I was. But I hadn't done anything. "Get out of my car" he yelled loud enough for just us to hear. "Go in there and tell them what a little bitch you are."

I hung my head, tears streaming down my face, reaching for the handle on the door, when he said "if you ever go in there and call my name", pulling back the hammer on the gun, "I shoot every rass person out here and kill miself." "Don't think that I am playing either, go in there and call me fucking name and see. Now get out!" Every hair on my body stood up, as I looked back at someone unworthy to be called human. I slammed the door with all my might; hoping to leave fear in the car. If I could somehow leave fear in the car, I'd have the courage to tell the authorities the whole truth and nothing but the truth.

He sped off while a staff member asked me some questions to help lead me in the right direction. Once I got to the right people they asked me a series of questions, or rather tried their hardest to get me to say Dwayne touched me. I kept telling them he didn't, all the while wondering how no one thought it odd that neither my father, nor any other guardian was there. All they wanted me to say was that Dwayne had committed a crime, unaware that the looney that dropped me off was the only guilty party. But I couldn't tell them that, so I kept insisting only a half truth, the truth that would keep my friend out of trouble.

As they probed and stuck and opened, silent tears ran down my face, not because of the pain of my still virgin vagina was suffering, but because of the wrongness in it all. The man that was supposed to protect and serve was himself the culprit. At the end of it all they gave me a white pill that was to cleanse any sperm from my body, only problem was there was none. That night I hated that monster more than I ever had before. The pills went in, and in the only words I can describe, felt like someone had a scissor inside of me, cutting away at my womb, as I twisted and cried in pain and agony.

There were only a few weeks left before our annual trip to the U.S. for the summer. If I could just hold out and hide myself from him a little longer, then it would all be over soon enough. The results wouldn't be in for a few weeks, which worked in my favor. Being uncertain of damaged goods he resorted to waiting to decide my ultimate fate I suppose.

Would you believe this psycho was in the house avoiding me? He would walk past me in the house as if I weren't there, rolling his eyes when we made eye contact, and all I could think was what a bitch! The only thing I saw was this man prepping me to be his woman, and I wasn't going to adhere to his twisted plans. It was a temporary paradise for me, but at least by the time the results came in it would be just about time to leave the island.

Suitcases packed outfits selected and still one week to go, outside I heard him howling my name but I refused to acknowledge him. I thought if I ignored him, he'd possibly go away, but he didn't. Instead he kept shouting, but not aggressively as I'd gotten accustomed to. As I approached the veranda, keeping my distance while trying to figure out what the story was behind the perverted smile on his face, no sooner than the thought left my head he blurted out "I'm sorry". Understanding the puzzled look on my face, he explained I was telling the truth. I asked with an attitude for him to be clear and tell me what was going on. "You were telling the truth, the results came back and you're still a virgin. I'm sorry I didn't believe you before". I assume in his head he thought his sweet talk actually meant something to me. He posted up on the truck so easy going, as if nothing happened and said, "I hope you can forgive me. I'm really sorry I didn't believe you, but you have to understand how it looked from my point of view". Played his old broken record about how he'd stop and get help, but I was over it and I knew he sensed that.

Finally at the airport saying what I thought for sure would have been our last goodbyes, my father leaned in close, and in a whisper said, "I dare you to go up there and call my name, using his body to hide his hand around my throat. I heard the point loud and clear, and thankfully I would have some time, comfort, and peace of mind to think long and hard.

Finding a way to tell my mom wouldn't be easy. She was never the bonding, sit down and talk type of mother. If there was no drama, gossip, or lies she couldn't relate. The perfect opportunity would have to present itself somehow.

We went through the first half of the summer as if all was well. Sundays we went to church, well everything was church related. Trips to the amusement parks, fun days in the park, Friday night hang outs, even the kids we hung with during the week went to church. Didn't mind though, it gave me a chance to be around kids my age, and for a little while just be normal. One thing I learned for sure while I was away, my mother worked really hard. During the week she held down a live in job, taking care of a lady who had a stroke, she was really kind towards us, even let us stay at work in the week with our mom. Well one evening as my mom prepared dinner, I figured that would be as good a time as any to ask her a few questions. See I couldn't just blab. I had to know for certain where her brain was and how she felt about these things. If she sent me back out of ignorance, blind to just how severe the situation really was, and told him she knew, we would have been DOA.

No, I had to be smart, pick at her brain a bit. "Mommy, is it ok for a father to kiss his daughter on the lips, even when they are big like me?" Thinking this woman would realize how off that question was, she simply mashed her potatoes and said, "No, nothing wrong with it if it's her father, he's just showing her love.

FUCK! This was not happening all over again. This answer was all too eerily similar to what I'd been told by that man. I repeated, on the lips, lips, lifting my finger to my lips, hoping to get her to just look in my eyes. I knew for sure if she looked in my eyes right in that moment, she would have seen, she would have known. Instead she just kept on cooking, never looking up she says, "Fathers and daughters kiss all the time."

What the hell was going on? Had all the adults in my life completely lost their parenting capabilities? I temporarily held my disheartenment to ask if I could stay there with her and go to school in America. She kept her head down, not saying a word, but after a series of my annoying questions she finally broke, telling me no. She reminded me that my eldest sister Marie was still in the process of filing her paper work for her permanent residence and that would slow things down. Giving her one last chance to see that I was begging her not to let me go back home I asked "please mommy, what if it is best for me that I stay here?" That moment I learnt that some people have children, while some are truly parents because all she said was, no! She never wondered why I was asking or saying these things or why I wanted so badly to stay, nothing. It became so clear to me right then that if I was going to win this, I'd have to do it all by myself.

One thing I still held as truth, that man was not climbing on top of me, I made up my mind I'd kill him dead in the action if he ever tried it.

Sadly I couldn't say anything to my mother; I'd thought her to be much smarter than she actually was. If she wasn't ready to keep us, and based on the answers to my question and answer session, I couldn't trust her to believe me or understand just yet. I spent the rest of the summer plotting, thinking, analyzing and most of all praying. I never believed in that stuff they spoke about in church, but in that moment I gave a chance to every god I'd learnt of in Religious Education class, promising anyone that granted me redemption my loyal following. Until he slipped up which I knew he would, I just had to get creative. Most of all I had to survive.

5

Going home was all bitter and no sweet. He had a smirk on his face the first time our eyes met again, a smirk that said I won, you are powerless and you know better than to have said anything. I smiled inside, because I had plans. His prized jewel would be taken away.

That night I put on 3 layers of everything. I figured since I was such a sound sleeper, it would take him some time to get through. A very tight jeans shorts as the final surprise should definitely slow him down.

It worked like a charm he got the first layer down, but by the time he got to the second layer, I felt a nudge, waking up to find my father half way past my thighs with the second pair of pajama pants in his grip. He dropped them then tip toed out the room as if he really thought I didn't see him. Could he really be serious? I didn't sleep the rest of that night. I just laid there, partially gloating over my small victory, if but for one night, on the other hand really coming to terms with what I was possibly up against. I gave in to the moment though and enjoyed feeling power, as though I was in charge and he had to hide from me.

The following morning I stared at him in disbelief, shaking my head, wondering how he had the ability to behave so normal. I asked him why he had been in my room the previous night. I asked, at too low of a point to really care. He froze, Jen froze, keta was somewhere far from the drama. "I heard you crying, as if you were having a nightmare, so I came in to check on you". "And the nightmare was in my pants?"

At this point I expected my head to be slapped off my body, but nothing happened. Instead he calmly faced me saying, "Mon, you know you sleep badly, I was just fixing your clothes". I looked over towards the other adult in the room wanting to ask, if she needed it to be any clearer than it was in that moment. I just couldn't understand why she wasn't helping me? What did she have to lose? As far as I'd hear her complain over the phone to friends and family, he wasn't even paying her properly. At that age sex was not a natural thought, and what I did not know was forcibly impressed upon me, so I never thought for a second that perhaps he'd been screwing her too. Things only got worse in the house each day, with little joy coming from my padding tactic still keeping him at bay, even if only for a few weeks.

My 13th birthday was around the corner, and the only wish I wanted, was a break from the horny boy I called my father. It remained just a wish though, as I soon realized I wasn't the only one anxiously awaiting my birthday. As soon as it hit, it was as if I'd begun sending out some stronger sense of woman essence or something of the sort because he amped way out of control. Things became so wacky in his behavior I started taking naps in one of the huge Julie mango trees that casted a huge shade in the yard. I took an old mattress from my baby crib and created a hideaway in the safety of the branches.

Even the neighbors began to notice the strange behaviors getting worse each day. Ms. Bev called me to her veranda to shed some light as to what was truly going over in my house. My mouth couldn't keep up with my brain, and by the time it did I was telling her about that very day. Everyone's face was in shock. "Mr. Doran doing what, Mr. Carlton shouted, as softly as he could. I nodded my head to confirm that what I had said was accurate and true. When they asked why I had been silent, and learned of the threats, they advised me to be careful and find a way to let my mother know once I left. Yet again no one was going to intervene on my behalf, for the same reasons I had not on my own behalf. A corrupted system, with too many broken links, the law wasn't sure to protect them. They reminded me to be careful about it, and that they were there for me if I really needed them, go figure.

All my lunch money was now being saved up to buy locks. The first one I put on felt like I was taking back my power, or at least control a bit of it. He was so angered by that first lock, he walked up and down the halls shouting, reminding us that this was his house, and no locks were going to stay on the door. I suppose he realized how shitty that made him look, because he ended up leaving me alone for some time.

That victory died at the beginning of the following school week, when I came home that Monday evening and my lock was missing. I didn't let it ruffle my feathers, and I didn't even bat an eye at him or that lock, for I made up in my mind I'd buy a lock every day for as long as it took for him to leave me alone.

I went without lunch for a few days to buy my locks, until I realized that the vendor we bought from by the school gate was always having so many orders thrown at him at once I could easily order food then ask for change, I did and it worked like a charm as the noise made it all too confusing. A skill that albeit not very honest, came in very handy when my father got pissed and started giving me less money to go to school with, barely having anything left over to buy even a Chicken Patty after bus fare. I didn't let him phase me though; I was determined to keep my virginity till I chose to give it away.

Unable to process the fact that I was winning at his sick little game, he began a huge argument one day over me showing insolence in keeping the locks on the doors. He said it showed disrespect to him in his own house. When Jennifer disagreed with him, all hell broke loose. She yelled over and over "Mr. Doran, you are a sick man, you're sick! "You need help, and you need it now". With that he died down, appearing to search his empty soul, but it was an act, a moment, a cycle that I was all too used to.

My good old prince charming ran into me one day while I was heading to school. It was the first time I'd really gotten the chance to vibe with him since the incident, as everyone in the tenement yard knew my face and heard what happened, I was scared they'd hate me, not knowing the story. After catching up and sharing a few laughs, he got serious, and then said he thought it was time to take the bastard out.

Dwayne asked me for every single detail of my father's evening after work, and I gave it to him. Later that evening I got a call that I should stay on the passenger side of the car when I opened the gates to let him in, because they'd be in the trees waiting. This was too surreal. Just like that, after all this suffering it was finally about to end? I couldn't believe it. Sure enough when I went to let him in I heard two guns hammer back, and my heart sank.

There in the mango tree I looked and saw Dwayne with his brother, ready to set me free, but my heart felt heavy and so much flashed through my mind all at once. One of the consequences if we went through would mean we'd be orphaned for some time. That was the easy part though, thinking of his blood on my shoulders, he was a monster, but I couldn't do it. I shook my head in a no motion, signaling to them that I changed my mind, and then stood on his side of the car as he drove up. They could kill him, but not on my watch, not while I was watching anyway. I guess that's why he spoiled us as kids, always went out of his way for us, because he knew how hard it would make this very moment for me. That night as I thought of how my chance was right there and how I gave it away, I held my pillow tight and cried. As I laid there wondering if I'd been stupid and deserved everything that was happening, something deep inside me told me that I made the right decision, that he'd get his soon enough. I felt it would be quite challenging but if I just kept making calculated moves, and keep trusting my gut, someway, somehow it was all going to work out in my favor.

All of this craziness led to new and disturbing behaviors from me, that I didn't even recognize myself anymore. Adding salt to the wound, not a soul ever thought to ask me any questions, and those who blatantly knew still batted their blind little eyes as if they saw nothing. I fought constantly at school with everyone and anyone; there was no person off limits to me. One particular already unpleasant day my English and form teacher decided to accept the temptation to fuck with me. We got in an argument which ended with her dumping the class' trash on my head, followed by me using her to mop the floor.

Man I took out all the frustration I was feeling for about a month or so on that woman. Luckily for me, the pastor's wife had a few choice words, letting me off the suspension hook. That hook went right out the window the following day, when some girl in my class tried to play me over not kissing some American boy's ass, and me serving her face to the metal desk. I was so out of control, but they wouldn't understand, I rarely had the chance to show them who I really was, I was too busy thinking about home to be a kid. I decided to keep this suspension to myself, after all if they were too busy to ask if all was well, or see the guilt on his face when he was there then fuck it, it wouldn't make a difference.

On my re-instatement day I knew I couldn't just waltz into the school yard without my parent or someone sent by them. I walked out to the Jamaica College bus stop, lunch money in hand, hoping to buy the right person for the part. After a few minutes a young man approached me, spliff behind his ear, ratchet knife in waist, hair braided, wearing a Rasta mesh vest walking his bike, I knew he'd help me out or at least want the money.

Sure enough he did and as we walked back to the school we recited some info I knew they'd ask him, and for $500 I bought me a cousin. I walked through the school gates with my chest puffed high, as if I'd won some victory over the dean, I was sure It'd be easy as 1,2,3. He regurgitated the lines we rehearsed, and his manners weren't too shabby either. At the end of the meeting Mrs. Finley the dean walked up to me and asked me to repeat where my father was, I repeated that he'd been stationed in Montego Bay for some time. She gave me an eye that clearly said she knew more than she was saying, smirked, and then dismissed me off to my homeroom.

There was a sense of pride all over my face as I gloated all the way there, really convinced I had pulled one over ole Finley's head. Just as I got settled into the school day, bragging to close friends I knew wouldn't say a word, a classmate told me Finley was looking for me by the office.

When I saw my father in the threshold of her office my blood went cold, if you cut me no blood would have escaped. My mouth hit the floor, while Ms. Finley stood there with an evil smirk on her face, like that of a wicked step mother. "Who is this Monique?" "My father" I replied. She asked me how he managed to get to Kingston from Mobay that fast, a question to which I had no answer. Ignorant to the fact the school had my father pretty much on speed dial; they called as soon as I walked away. My father had his fists balled up so tightly I thought for sure he'd break his own fingers. He looked deeply into my eyes as he bit his bottom lip wanting so badly to fuck me up, but he didn't hit me as he normally would. He told me that he would take care of me when I got home. I prayed and hoped that the dean would have just asked me if everything was ok at home, but then I really wasn't sure any more if I'd really have the courage to say something had she asked. But I still wished somehow she could have sensed that something was terribly off balance in his tone of voice towards me, his stare and body language, as far as I saw were all telltale signs. She could see everything else, why couldn't she see the problem behind the problem.

My punishment for embarrassing him as he called it was to wash all his buttoned shirts he wore to work and court for a whole week. I wondered and questioned if he perhaps saw me as his mate or equal.

My out of control behavior began getting me into a whole lot of trouble, but I also met new people as well. So many people knew of me because of my behavior, all except one person I spotted while my father was pretending to be a father for the dean. His name was Andre, the Head Boy of the school, perfectly pleated and iron, not a hair out of place. He had kind eyes, and a welcoming smile, nerdy and all about the books, in his 11th grade year of school. Maybe it was the fact that we were total opposites but something inside of me assured me I'd be safe with him.

I didn't know him but I trusted him, I had to. I stalked him, made a prey of him, always watching without him even noticing. If he was going to break my virginity, it couldn't just be sex, there had to be some beautiful story behind it, perhaps me confessing why I was doing this, and him wanting to rescue me. I became his friend on purpose, regardless of the fact that he was 17 and I was 13, we became really great friends. We spoke on the phone after school just about every day, each convo left me in awe of this young man, as he never once brought up the topic of sex. Even when I tried, he would tell me I was a beautiful young lady, but too young, his answer would always be no. Every guy I'd met so far had more morals than my father did. I took no for an answer, but temporarily, remaining in very close friendship, determined this would be the person no matter what!

Things at home intensified. We entered what I called the final stages of this beast' plans, things became really heated in the house, arguments were no longer in a hushed tone, I yelled out all the things that I needed him to stop doing, loudly without care, I just didn't care anymore. I lashed back, telling him he could kill us all I simply didn't care enough to carry that burden anymore. We would play the routine of I'll change, I'll get help, but the routine was old, and lost its effect. I was tired of the way things were. It was either going to be leave or die.

As if things weren't already way past the limit they should be, he decided to add his penis to his sick game. Whenever he left work at nights, we'd have to collect our lunch money from him the following morning. Well I had to collect our lunch money. The first morning it happened I walked in his room said my good mornings as I always did, but this morning something was different, his dick was standing at full attention as he laid there under the sheets, showing no form of apology. I stopped in my tracks, speechless, staring in disbelief. "Why are you like this?" I asked as he barely attempted to grab a pillow to cover his nastiness. He walked to the nightstand on the opposite side of the bed, grabbed his pants that held his wallet, taking his sweet slow time to in getting out the money, and spitefully going even slower while counting it, all the while standing there with the pee hole of his boxer exposing a half of his erected penis shaft. I tried my hardest to look everywhere but down, as he took his diligent time before finally handing me the money. This happened every nightshift's morning, each occasion more blatant that the time before. I updated Jen about his latest taunting, asking, and begging for the chance to go report him. "We'll get him help was the only answer I ever managed to get out of her. When the situation hit its peak I was seeing his bare naked penis, now feeling scared somewhat,

I remained aware of my position in his room and always set myself up to exit. After numerous mornings of throwing up in my mouth, and after fighting to keep the thought of the ugly bump on top of his manhood out of my head during classes, I told Jennifer I'd rather walk to school, stay hungry or hustle my food, walk back home, before I went back in that room another morning under those circumstances. She assured me she would make arrangements for me to get my money for the entire week on Sunday evenings from her. When I asked again why she wouldn't just report him, she told me to trust her as best as I could, telling me to remember that he was a sick man who wasn't afraid to die and take us with him.

He went crazy that week! I came home one evening to find the door to my room off its hinges and laying on one of the beds. He was screaming from his room on the top of his lungs, that it was his house; he was going to do as he damn well pleased, with whomever he pleased.

Instantly my blood ran cold, and all I could do was weep loudly. For just that moment I no longer cared, he had won. What else was I to do? I tried everything. I was only 13 years old, why should I bear this burden, I thought. Then I remembered of the story of my birth, at least what they'd told me all my life.

Apparently on September 13th, 1985, a Friday morning, my mother went into what everyone thought would be a typical healthy birthing. My head crowned, the doctor got a grasp, and then suddenly I decided I wasn't ready, I returned to the comforts of the womb. On Monday September 16th, with my mother emptied of all protective fluids, and the possibility of my death, was now being rushed by ambulance to deliver by C-section. While en route to the clinic, I came without notice and so on purpose. I realized how intentional I was, for such a soul must be here for some greater purpose than to simply whither at the hands of this man. I also came to the reality that all the adults playing a role in my life were all losing their minds and that I had to protect both my little sister and myself at all costs. Worst case scenario in my head, was him diverting from me to baby sis, leaving me thankful I was the thick mature one, while she looked like a twig. For her sake most of all I would fight to get out.

Despite my layered approach, I still fell into deep sleeps, waking up to find a sticky substance in my vagina, which were further confirmed each time by his sick stories of last night. Coming to a level of comfort knowing that he was not after my sister, refusing to continue to stay in the room without a door, I began sleeping in Jen's bed. I had to make him slip up; I also knew he would follow his candy wherever it went. A few nights went by with him surprisingly fighting the urge, but by the 4th day he did exactly what I knew and hoped he'd do, mess up.

Snuggled up behind Jen, feeling the safest I'd felt in a really long time, I felt a pinch on my nipple, but thought for sure I had to be dreaming. Now I'm sure everyone can relate to being in a dream that feels more like an outer body experience, and that's exactly what I thought was happening. I refused to wake up; convincing myself he would never have the balls or audacity to be that brazen. A hard pinch on my nipples gave me what I needed to open my lazy eyes, when I did, all I could do was yell "Jen daddy have his hands on my nipples" repeatedly.

He was leaning over Jennifer to get to me, hands still on my chest. It took her a minute, but when she finally realized what was really happening, she jumped to her feet "Mr. Doran what the hell wrong wid you man? Jesus Christ Mr. Doran why don't you just stop this shit? You're sick! You need to just stop this shit now, it's gone too far now!" Still in a daze of disbelief, I slowly rose up from the bed placing my exposed breast back in my night gown, saying, asking, screaming, "What the hell is wrong with you?" This man just stood there with a stupid grin on his face, finally opening his mouth to say "I was just waking her up to get ready for school." "By squeezing my nipple" I shouted. I was done, over this. That's really all this stupid asshole had to say? I was living in a certified mad house, with mad neighbors, attending a mad school, I even started to wonder if it was me that, maybe I was overthinking this entire situation and everything was quite normal.

Hell no! I knew all of this was wrong, no way in hell was my father's name going to be in my virginity story, unless it was of him trying to dismantle me once he found out I'd robbed him the chance.

No one seemed to be able to stop this man, I became so desperate for someone to hear or listen that one day I decided to vent while with Ms. Campbell, a close friend of my mother from church, so close to us she was almost like an acting mother, well at church anyway. Standing by the church gate, alone and away from the usual crowd who were always happy for a lift in my father's pick-up truck to Crossroads after church, in a whispered tone I asked if I could trust and confide in her about something. Sensing something was wrong she gave me her undivided attention, and no sooner than the yes rolled from her tongue, I unloaded.

She was speechless for a while, breaking her silence with the last words I'd ever expect to come out of her mouth of all people. "Monique that can't be true, I refuse to believe that, no not Mr. Doran, he wouldn't do that." Any external flame of hope that was keeping me alive had certainly been snuffed out. I asked how she could really not believe me, asked her what reason I would have to make up such a lie against my father? She told me that I was a trouble maker, that I was known for lying, while he was known for being a great father and a good man. A man such as my father could never commit the acts of which I spoke. I walked away, losing another bit of faith, comforting myself with the thought that it was a last ditch effort anyway. I'd gotten so accustomed to the adults in my life failing me, but I thought for sure she if no one else, she would believe me. She was always so kind to us, so loving and caring, but sadly all she could see were my bad behaviors, but couldn't see what I was saying, wouldn't even try.

6

Andre's walls slowly began to fall thanks to my charm, or as he put it, my very mature way of reasoning and my logics were well beyond my years. I didn't bluntly tell him what was going on, or what role he was playing but I dropped hints. Whenever we spoke, I deliberately shifted the tone into a sexual tone, getting more blatant each time. I even told him that it was necessary that he broke my virginity, but it took physical hangouts, sharing personal moments for him to finally open to the thought of granting me my wish. Finally after I broke all barriers, he told me he didn't understand why it was so important, but the young lady I seemed to be must mean it was important to me, and agreed to help me. He wanted no drama, and privacy, as his head boy status was at stake, losing it would just ruin him and I'd never let that happen, not if I could help it anyway. I kept our relationship a secret, not a soul besides us was in on our secret.

All in perfect timing though I suppose as the camel's back was broken when what appeared to be my father completely losing his mind. Frustration and a few drinks unleashed the darkest depths in that man. He came home yelling after me all around the yard, cursing, until finally finding me in the closet. He swung the door open, raised his hand, made a click sound and before I realized what was really happening, there was a gun by my head. He felt on me, grabbing all my private parts, stripping me of any and all pride. I felt so violated, wanting so badly to run to the knife I kept under my mattress in case he ever tried to pin me down. I screamed out for Jennifer, though by that time I had begun to wonder why I even bothered. By the time she came storming through the door, he already walked away, smirking, taking a deep breath, inhaling what he had taken from my body. I fell to the floor and cried, just laid there and bawled my eyes out.

The next day at school I approached Andre, telling him it had to be that weekend. After that last episode I was sure what happened next would either end with me luckily killing him first or him killing me after he had his way. It was planned with the very last minute detail included. I first thought to use youth fellowship on a Friday night at church as my way to get it done, but my sister was too young and simply wouldn't understand there would be too many questions to answer. No, it would have to be a Saturday morning, as going to the library to complete projects were the norm. It worked out even better as we were allowed to go to the game arcade for an hour or so once we got all our information early enough. I would photocopy all the info I needed as soon as I got there then found my way to Prince Charmin's house.

On Saturday May 1st, 99 that is exactly what I did. He lived on a rough side of town known as "Waterhouse" in Kingston, and though it was my first visit, I was no stranger to its name. From all the news, my father and just about every person had to say concerning this garrison, I had no right being there, but this was more than well worth it. There was no way I was going to lose my chance at choice. This chance to create my own story, with his word that all would be perfectly fine I pressed on and followed him through a huge zinc gate. Inside was a hidden world of small and medium 1-2 bedroom houses, tenement homes. Everyone stood around staring and whispering, as if they knew what I was there to do. Once inside his home I took my shoes off and made myself comfortable while he offered me something to drink. Titanic played, but we talked through most of it, connecting on a much deeper level, leaving me even more thankful for what would be the story behind the story.

Halfway through the movie he asked me what time I had to be home, as sort of nudge to find out what was up. Thanks to the route between our houses and the speed at which the bus drivers drove, it would be a short ride home and extra time to claim my victory at last. I'd never thought of losing my virginity before all of this mess, but given the circumstances I was just happy to be able to choose at the very least to have it be with someone I respected. In a most gentle tone he asked if I wanted to finish watching the movie or commence our plans. On the inside, I felt young, shy, reserved and inexperienced, yet ready and determined. He took me and laid me on the bed taking his time, constantly asking if I was sure I was ready. He tried for hours with no success.

If you've ever watch the Titanic, then you know how very long it runs, it ended and restarted and still nothing. Overcome with emotion I began crying, and he stopped to ask if it hurt or if I'd changed my mind, but that was not the case, I was just scared as hell that he'd get annoyed and change his mind. He took me into his arms with such care, then asked, "this is really important to you isn't it?" He cradled me tighter, and then whispered in my ear, this will hurt, but if you are ready I can get it done. I braced myself and as gently as he could, with one mighty push it as over. I screamed into the pillow to dull the pain, but to also celebrate a victory. I had robbed that bastard of the ultimate prize, I beat him at his own game taking what he could never have again, winning a battle at long last. Anything after this I could handle, but decided to fight my hardest to still somehow have the last laugh by leaving alive and untouched.

I walked to the bathroom proudly as every eye that was in that yard was centered on me, and I didn't care one bit. There was no power or person that could undo what had been done. If I had nothing else I had this story at the very least.

I told no one about that Saturday, no one at all, so there was definitely some explanation needed when my father approached me the following Monday morning. He leaned on the van smiling a cool cat sarcastic kind of smile, motioning for me to join him. When I did he let me know that he knew. I played fool to what he was saying, asking him to explain himself so I could understand. As far as I saw it he didn't even know Andre existed, so he could never be talking about me losing my virginity.

Oh honey, the look I saw in his eyes told me all hell was about to break loose, but I had no idea just how much. With a sort of jealous, cynical grin he blurted, "You went and had sex huh? I have a flight this afternoon to go and see your mom, when I see her she'll know too." With my own sarcastic attitude I simply waved my hand for him to go ahead, and get out of my way so I could get to school. He shared a few choice words, and told me how I'd let him down, that he had plans for me, for us, and how I'd ruined everything. I asked why he never reported Dwayne, all the while still playing clueless, as I hadn't revealed any info. But I didn't care enough to reason things out with him. As a matter a fact that's exactly the thing I needed him to do, tell her.

I figured or at least prayed to all the universal powers that existed that my mother had enough sense to ask him how he came by the information. Once she asked that question she'd be forced to call me, asking how he knew and who I'd told.

The phone rang, I picked up, "You dirty little piece of shit, you slut dog". I took the receiver from my ear, staring at it in disbelief of what I was hearing from what sounded to be the voice of my mother on the other line. This couldn't be the mother that thought she was a Christian and forced me to go to church every Sunday, no I must have been confused. I placed her voice next to my ear once more to check what was happening for sure; sure enough she was still there calling me every horrible name she could find in the book. I removed the receiver once more, staring at it with disbelief. With tears streaming I screamed as loud as I could. I was done and over it. How could she not ask me that question? She had one job to do, ask me a question that should come natural to any mother with a sense of maternal love. When I got tired of her screaming and the name calling I finally faced her and prepared for her to tear me apart.

"Monique, what did you do? What's his name, how old is he, where does he live? I'm putting his ass in prison!" After the numbness of the shock wore off enough for me to speak, I asked her the blatant question she should have asked him, how he knew, then informed her that I hadn't told a soul. She paused, realizing I suppose that truly there would only be one honest answer to that question. That she should have somehow saw the signs as a mother, been more involved, but then I guess one doesn't naturally, nor should have to worry about a father doing anything but protecting a child, none the less the burden of guilt was there to be shared and she definitely realized that in her answer. What she could have done but didn't was to then in that moment choose to ask, instead she bypassed my question, as if it had not even been uttered from my lips. She resumed her name calling, I no longer cared and felt defeated, which allowed me to become weak and surrender all the info on Dre. By the end of that night he hated me and wished we'd never met. He was in a whole lot of mess trying to help me solve my own problems. I begged his forgiveness but could easily understand his unwillingness to do so. I knew she was just upset and wouldn't really hurt him; he didn't, so hating me was definitely tolerable.

With hope, my best friend and my last foreseeable avenue of escape gone, I delighted in the fact that I had at least altered the story in my favor. The future was unclear to me, but one thing held steady no matter what, my vision of winning.

I asked Jen after it was all done how she could just sit by and not say anything at all knowing all she did. "I just don't have enough blatantly proof to say anything right now". Fear of his fellow officers I could understand, but here, now, in the most perfect time to be of help she remained silent. She made it so clear to me in doing so that there was something going on between her and my father.

I was no stranger to finding my father on top of the help, while getting up to get milk at 1:00 in the morning. My mother's complaints and fights with him about those brazen acts of adultery were also very common in the house. Hell this man has tried to sleep with just about every female on my mother's half of the family, so the thought of sex between them was very plausible. It was the only reason I could think of, as to why she'd stand before me telling me she had no proof.

That week gave me the courage to say enough! I had grown too tired of playing his little mind games, making the decision right then and there, that summer when I got away, I would not under any circumstance not tell my mother blatantly what was happening. The burden had become too much to bare, if he were to kill me, at least I'd die much lighter and eased of my load.

Smoking weed was my sanity for the next few months, and anywhere outside the house was my haven. I hung with girls from the garrisons, whom I admired greatly, for they had not been so sheltered and well coursed in looking out for themselves. I observed in silence, as they taught me the road codes without them even knowing it. I played hooky most days and often the third wheel for my new friends as they went on their sexcapades; I was never really interested in having sex again. Sure it had been an awesome experience and all, but my intention over the next few months was survival and survival only. The weed helped me escape the reality of feeling like I was really becoming his woman, as things got so bad at the house we began arguing outside, always sounding like sour lovers. I was living with a time bomb that was sending me signals it could go off at any moment without notice.

Summer just wouldn't arrive fast enough. With his chance at his grand prize robbed from him, he was left without a goal, which made him miserable, as we all know misery loves company. He taunted me day and night. Each day he formulated a new way in which he was going to kill me. Reminded every day of his true thoughts of me and the slut he believed me to be. Still it remained, I would always have the upper hand, and I took from him what he could never in all his powers have again, created my own memory, and for just a day, in one moment, gave ME POWER. It was worth everything, and played out exactly as hoped. To him I was now damaged goods, I had lost the value I once held, which caused him to lose his thrill and interest in me, or so I hoped anyway. Either way for the moment, I only had to worry about words, watch for signs this crazy fuck was going to make a move to end my life, and how I was going to break all this to my mother. I practiced every day, imagining her grief stricken face, hoping she didn't have a heart attack or that her pressure wouldn't go through the roof, most of all that she'd even believe me.

7

Our departure date arrived shortly after school had let out. Summer of 99 was finally here, and I just knew it had brought my deliverance. When we arrived at the airport, he performed his routine threats, the routine stare down, and the old gun clutching. My reaction however was anything but the same old routine. Fear was no longer a factor. For the first time I truly gave zero little duckling fucks as to what he would do to me, and the dry, hard cold stare I gave him said that loud and clear. I sashayed away feeling confident, giving thanks that I had been given the chance to make it off the island before he took the opportunity to force himself inside of me, even worst to live with his blood on my shoulder.

Coming up with scenarios of me breaking the news to my mother were the only images I could visualize. Would she grab me and hug me, console and comfort, or would she knock the life out of me convinced I was telling a lie. Would she leave the country and kill him with her own hands? Would she get him arrested? Would she even be shocked at all?

It so happened that the client she took care of decided to vacation at their Jersey beach house that summer, this meant that her son who had accompanied us, would be spending more time with his dearest mother, meaning I would have more alone time with my own. It was a beautiful big blue house, sitting just off the shore of the beach. There was a cozy little patio out the back that my mother loved to sit and watch the water, not being a fan of being in the water.

One evening as we sat out on the deck enjoying the hot Jersey sun, the perfect moment presented itself when they informed us they were going for a walk down the board walk. My mother only being comfortable in her own culture told them to go ahead without her. When they extended the invitation to my sister and me, I seized the moment to be alone with my mom. I told baby sis to bring me something after politely asking to stay at the house.

"I'm sorry mommy." The silence between us finally broke. Sure she had shared a few words with me, but as you can imagine any mother learning what she did and not sharp enough to catch the real story, she wanted as few exchange of words between us as possible. When she finally broke her silence she asked what it was that I was sorry for. I told her that I was sorry for the way my actions made her feel, that I was truly sorry for making her lose hope in me but that I wasn't sorry for breaking my virginity. When I made that bold of a statement everything that she had bottled up for the past three months came like a rushing river. I allowed her to unload, never interrupting her, and just as she got through calling me every name in the book, I whispered just loud enough for her to hear, I had to. She paused for a moment, frowned her face demanding that I repeated myself. As dry eyed as ever I looked her square in the eyes and said "I had to break my virginity!" Realizing that she was fixing to whoop me properly, thinking I was being fresh, I continued yelling "or else daddy would have done it instead".

Thinking the chair was still beneath her she attempted to sit, but caught herself right before she hit the floor. With a chilled stare on her face she asked what I meant by what I said whilst trying to find the chair with her hands, not wanting to take her eyes off me. "Daddy has been trying to have sex with me and just about everyone but you know about it. They've been telling me not to tell you yet, that I had to be careful". Her ear got more than its full share of why they'd said that and everything that had happened up to that moment.

After sitting with a blank clueless stare for what seemed like an eternity, she jumped from the chair, grabbing her crotch, wailing as a woman who had suffered the loss of a child or someone very dear. "Mi pussy, Mi pussy", she shouted at the top of her lungs, just jumping and hopping all over the place in disbelief of what I'd just said. She then began repetitively chanting that she knew something was wrong, she just knew something was wrong! "Why didn't you say something to me?" I reminded her about the part of the story where he threatened to kill everyone, and pulling a gun on me in the closet. Then I asked her just what she meant by the statement she made about knowing that something wrong was going on?

She told me of a time when I was 11 years old, and he had been visiting her, when she overheard him on the phone telling me that I was to remember that he left me in charge till he came back. She said she thought it odd that he would tell a child my age something like that, especially when Jennifer was there as an adult. "Why didn't you ask me if anything strange was happening then if you felt something was off?" She dismissed the notion that anything was wrong, because of how he had spoilt us. Everyone knew when we were younger, he sort of gave us too much power as children, not correcting us as times he should have, but I guess now I could see he had begun his preparations from even then. I tried my best to understand from her point of view, but in that moment I just couldn't, I believed it was her duty as my mom to be so connected with me, she would have felt all that I felt.

We sat outside talking for what felt like hours. Just as we were about to wrap things up, she came with a twist I did not see coming. She leaned in as if she were coming to hug me, then whispered softly, "Monique mek we sweep it unda the rug. Some things are best kept as family secret. No need letting it out, it will only do more bad than good to the family if we report or talk about it". "What! You mean to tell me you don't care? We're not going to have him arrested or anything?"

She said the same old excuse I had gotten so damn tired of hearing that the law looked out for the law; she also repeated that she thought the only thing that could come of it would be shame and disgrace on the family. "I will get you and Nak up here to live in a short time, you'll just have to play humble for a while, act as if you never said a word to me. I know it won't be easy, but it's the only way to get you up here safely." I reminded her of the fact that we were already there with her, already safe, why compromise that? Surely she could call and put him on some pedophile watch list, as I had seen in the movies. She simply continued to explain all the reasons we couldn't stay now, including the fact that she had nowhere for us to stay, the lawyer would need time to get us documents to enroll in school, most of all that she didn't want to spoil her own filing process, as it would only delay us. She asked me to be patient, humble and just give her some more time. Time however was a precious commodity I couldn't afford: no time to go back home, time to think, time to come to terms with what was coming out this woman's mouth. Hell I was still stuck in time where she told me to sweep it all under the rug.

That summer we secretly planned and plotted everyday as to how she would send for us at the end of December once school was out. We were to keep him thinking it was just a trip to go see the snow and experience our first Christmas in America. Though I was hurt by my mother's words and reaction to the situation, and even though the plan meant I could end up in grave danger, or worse yet dead, it was hope, my only hope, so I decided to go along with it as best as I could. I knew it would take every bit of strength I had in me to survive.

My mother seemed a bit changed after all had been revealed to her, well I guess as anyone should expect. I saw disappointment, a little sadness, maybe even a spark of envy, but never did I see shock. It's as if she knew it was always possible, but never really expected it to manifest. "Why are you not shocked, why are you so calm about everything?" I asked her one afternoon. She motioned for me to join her where she was sitting, then proceeded to tell me of a story about my father she learnt a long time ago. She said when she met my father, he was dating a teacher, and my mother herself had been married to her first husband as well. My father's common law wife had a sixteen year old daughter whom he impregnated around the time she became pregnant with me. The mother of the girl took her to have the baby aborted and was done with my father. She also told me stories of him molesting a very close family member when he was a teenager.

When I learned this info I was stuck at a loss for words. I had found out from my own mother that my father was an official pedophile and apparently a "family ram". I thought I most definitely couldn't return now, even more so because the man wasn't afraid to die. I felt like David standing up to Goliath, with only a sling and a stone, hoping for one good hit.

After we returned home I kept a smile on my face that hid perfectly the secret plans my brain was conjuring daily. I behaved as if all was still the same, being sure not to ruffle his feathers; the situation was much too fragile to cause any unnecessary drama, and thankfully he had gotten over the hunt stage, and I had the means to surviving his taunting stage. I even did my best to keep my mouth silent as he filled my ears with his garbage in the mornings. I stayed hidden in the trees when he was home, even got the girls football team up and running again at school so I could have an excuse to be home late. I asked my sister to sleep beside me at nights making her somewhat aware of the situation at hand, she was much too young, too innocent, to bare this burden. I separated myself from all my schoolmates and neighbors, some of whom had known me since birth. The jovial little girl that everyone knew was no more and a soldier of some sort had emerged.

Something snapped in him one day, as if he could sense that something was off, or his pedophilic senses were tingling, because as I sat in the living room, unbothered, expecting his usual shenanigans, he blurted, "You told your mother about us?" I asked what in the hell he was talking about, unsure and trying to see if he was trying to pick our brains. "You all think that I am stupid? You told her and now she's taking you away from me in December?" When I asked where he'd gotten an idea like that, he revealed that my mother made him aware that she wanted us for the holidays, so I played cool and behaved as if it was the first time I'd heard any of it. Somehow he felt we were lying, as if his gut told him he would not be seeing us for a long time once we left. With all the convincing I could muster, I nudged him into believing that it was just a trip that came about because we mentioned how lovely it would have been to experience the snow. Deep down I wanted to tell him to fuck off and indeed we were leaving, but I understood that when your hand is in the lion's mouth, you gotta take your time and ease it out.

It was late November, and I just had to keep my distance from him for another couple of weeks, then my problems would be permanently fixed. But he was relentless, turning up the heat, becoming more aggressive by the day, no bolder man could you have found if you were looking. He went on his long speeches more often about this being his house and that he intended to run it, not run around it. He made it clear that he had no intentions on asking permission for what was already his. Jennifer tried reasoning with him, showing him all that was at stake, and all he stood to lose that he was hurting and scarring me for life. That only seemed to make it worse; he went into full crazy after that. He taunted me day in and day out about the many ways he was going to take pleasure in eating my pussy before I left for good. I would stand there feeling every muscle of his tongue on my skin, sometimes leaving me hoping I'd piss him off enough he'd end up killing me. This beast was a really sick sack of shit, the kind that should have been flushed down a toilet, splattered on some sheets or aborted. He was an abomination to children everywhere. The only way to stay alive was to convince him I wasn't leaving for good and play his little fantasy games as safely as I could, and before I knew it December had shown her beautiful face.

It really hadn't even dawned on me until end of year exams had begun and we were planning for our farewell fete, the last time we'd see a lot of the people we knew for a really long time.

I was going to miss them all, my gang, the teachers, even the ones I'd terrorized, and feeling devastated that I couldn't tell them what was going on. I wouldn't even get the chance to stay in touch with any of them. It was a small price to pay for getting out of hell.

Packing my suitcase and seeing all the clothes scattered on the floor gave me a most genius idea to prove to Jennifer that it was all true. See I needed her to see with her own two eyes before we left so she knew without a shadow of doubt. The clothes scattered out like that would hide her perfectly under the bed, as my father did his dirty deeds. When I brought the plan to her she thought it a genius one and agreed to it immediately. It would work perfectly because us being kids it was usual to get really excited, tired, and then pass out sleeping, with all the clothes scattered till the next day.

That night we set the trap, littering just about every piece of clothing from all the drawers in the room, Jen positioned herself under the bed, ready and waiting for him to walk through the door in about 10 mins or so.

Well they say the average person falls asleep within ten minutes, and this must be true, because by the time my father came in to complete our plans, I'd been knocked out cold. I hadn't realized I'd dozed off until I heard shouts from Jennifer startling me back to reality.

"Mr. Doran, no! Mr. Doran, no!" "What happened?" I screamed at Jennifer, mad at myself for falling asleep but somewhat happy because I wouldn't have the memory, I begged and demanded all at the same time to know what she saw, but all she could do was shake her head and cry. For the first time I saw in her eyes that she really just understood, just how truthful I was being, and just how serious it all was. Trying one last time to get her to fill me in, she dismissed me, telling me that she could never speak what she just saw, ever! I pulled up my underwear, and then headed to the bathroom so I could get the sticky substance from between my legs.

Her eyes told me her world would never be the same, that whatever she saw would impact her memory forever. With all the heaviness my heart felt for the pain my father was causing in everyone's life, I was filled with joy that I now had an eye witness to his crimes. I finally exposed him for the monster he truly was, from here on out she was solely responsible for me getting off that island as my acting guardian. Another triumph in my favor, all I had to do now was wing it out for the another couple weeks, then my freedom would be waiting on the other side, finally saying goodbye to his hell.

He scorned me, rarely ever speaking to me. I was destroying everything he'd hope to accomplish. Robbed him of his goal, left him with no purpose, then exposed him, oh he was mf pissed. That was quite fine with me though, if there was even an hour's break from him, then he could keep it up all the way to my departure date, which was right around the corner. I decided to enjoy my last days creating happy memories with friends I wouldn't see for a very long time.

Before I knew it the end of school year fete had arrived. I felt so much sadness that all my teachers and schoolmates didn't get the chance to know the good and love in me. After enjoying my last moments with friends, roaming the halls of Mona High one last time, thankful for its existence and the people that had changed my life one way or another, whether they'd known of not, I went to pay Mrs. Finley one last visit to say goodbye, but also to retrieve a CD player that was confiscated earlier that year.

As she handed it over, I told her I thought she should know I was leaving for good over the break. Contrary to what I expected, she handed me the device, stared me in the eyes, and then said I'm glad you're leaving. I asked if I'd been that horrible of a person while I was there, to which she answered no. "I'm just glad you're leaving". She left me puzzled by her comment and I wondered what she was insinuating. Before I could ask what she meant by all her words, she asked if I was going to be living with my mother, when I told her yes, she breathed a sigh of relief, saying she was very happy for me. She told me that she suspected something was not quite right at home. She couldn't understand how I'd change so drastically in such a short period of time. She also said my father behaved very odd whenever they asked if everything was ok at home, drifting his eyes everywhere as to not make eye contact.

In that moment, I swear if I was cut I wouldn't have bled. I realized though that my salvation was drawing nigh, making it that much easier to forgive her neglect. I admitted to her that what she believed all along was correct, not giving her too much, but covering enough ground to catch her up. She gave me some sympathy, but all I left with was my belongings. Sympathy couldn't help, and though I appreciated it, action would have helped so much more, and then walked through the gates for the last time, for a long while.

8

December 17th 1999, was a day that permanently changed and shaped my life. Finally the day had come for me to leave all that horror behind, start new, and somehow, if possible, pretend it was a just a really bad dream, maybe even forget. Our bags were packed, outfits selected, and all our goodbyes were said. Time remained the only element between me and freedom, until about 8am. Basking in my victory, I hadn't realized he'd been speaking until the word passport and lost really permeated my daydream bubble. When I snapped out of it completely I realized that he'd really said that he lost my passport at the mechanics shop. Keeping my cool, understanding this was just some last ditch effort I played along asking what he was talking about.

He explained that he took the car for a tune up at Mabootu's, just to ensure that there were no hiccups on the way to the airport, then that morning had noticed that the book was missing. "Why was my passport in the van, but not keta's? Why was it even in there from the start?" His lame story had something to do with wanting to have all the documents in the van so we couldn't forget them. Seeing his antics and smelling his bullshit a mile away, I yelled at him that I was not in the mood for his foolishness. My book was only good to me, the upgraded system made the "Bandooloo" business more complex, and the timing was all too convenient. Worst part is this eediot truly expected me to believe that lame old story. How many times we traveled before, and the passports were always remembered. "Why didn't you have both of the books together?" Unfearful as to what his answer was going to be, the mother fucker in me rose up; she'd just about had enough of the bullshit and went straight for the jugular. "Listen I'm tired of going through this, with you. You are a sick man, and you need help! I I'm leaving the island, by will or by force.

Shock covered his face; he couldn't believe what had come out my mouth, hell I couldn't believe that happened. In a soft, calm voice he said, "Ok Mon we'll go find your book".

We, what did he mean by we? He said we'd go to the shop together so he could ruff the guys up till one of them spoke. But he was doing the ruffing up, the only we that needed to happen, was when we were driving to the airport. He threatened that getting into the van was the only way I'd ever see my passport again, so reluctantly I jumped in.

Something just did not feel right, but it was worth the risk if it meant I'd be free.

Ten minutes into our drive, sitting at a red light and staring at the huge Eastwood Park church that sat at the corner, remembering the teacher I'd whooped, as her husband was the pastor, wondering if perhaps karma was being revengeful for all the mean things I had done, or perhaps it was from a lifetime before, whatever the reason, this was no just punishment, simply torture. So silently in my heart I prayed that if it were something of the sort I'd be redeemed or that some miracle or the intervention of a mythical being would be so kind as to free me. As I prayed, it's as if some intuitive force answered, telling me it would all work out in my favor, but also that some physical showdown would be my last penance.

As the light changed and the vehicle lunged back to move forward, he interrupted my peace to tell me what I already knew, "Mon I know who has your passport." "Yes of course you do you, because you have it! I may be young, but as you must realize by now, not even close to stupid, just give me my things and let be on my way". His voice grew softer than before, "Ok Mon, you're right, I do have it, words that sent a rush of relief over me, but only a little and a very temporary one. I was happy to know it wasn't really stolen, but now I had to retrieve it from this monstrous villain. "But you have to do something for me before you leave, one last favor, then I will no longer stand in the way of you leaving if that is really what you want." What the hell did he mean if that is what I wanted, he had broken all the levels of sanity I could imagine.

" Let me eat your pussy, and then I will give you what you desire."

This man couldn't have been serious really? He spoke so casually, drove in such a calm unbothered manner I had no choice but to wonder if he was even aware of the words that just left his lips. "Hell no! Are you crazy? What is wrong with you daddy?" Placing emphasis on the word daddy, hoping it would resurrect him from the deep sleep he had to have been in, bringing back to life the real father I once knew, but sadly that didn't work. "It won't be that bad. Once I'm done then you can go, I promise".

Tears seemed to have been my best and most consoling friend and as expected they came rushing down my face uncontrollably. For the first time I told him verbally to his face just how much I hated, despised and wanted him dead, but he felt nothing, it had no effect on him. The plan was to call me into his room under the pretense that he was going to apologize for everything that he'd done wrong. He said if I just kept silent, everything would be ok.

Putting my emotional thoughts away, I went into survival mode. The fact was there was an airplane scheduled to leave the airport later that evening bounded for Florida. The other fact I held true was that I was going to be on there one way or another. For the moment I could just let him think he had won, giving me time to think of as many possible ways to get out of this alive and in one piece, maybe even untouched. I nodded my head yes, which was greeted which a smile that still makes me cringe. As he smiled he reached in his pocket, when his hand resurfaced, my ticket to freedom was there, so close in my reach, yet so very, very far away.

After he finally went in his room to prepare for his sick fantasy, I took the first chance I'd been given to share with Jennifer what his twisted plans were. By this time I'm feeling like the character that just never seems to learn, quite often making the same mistake, mine trusting the same folks that appeared to be helping.

She was my only hope at the moment, so together Jennifer and I planned and plotted.

I would go in the room as planned, get his guard down, and somehow convince him to give me the book as "brawta" or security. Once it was in my possession I'd yell out for Jen who would run in and save the day. A simple brilliant plan indeed, until we executed it.

This was too real. Here I was a 14 year old child, plotting how to get away from my father, who wanted to have oral sex with me. It felt like I was in one of those spy movies, wishing and praying the director would yell cut already.

A short while after we concretized our plan, he shouted for me to come to his room, his signal as the cue to execute his plans. I looked in Jen's eyes with a look of desperation. I had to explain to her without words just how badly I needed her to not fuck this one up.

Once I was in the room he began to say some jibber jabber loudly, about how sorry he was for all that had happen and how he wished he could have done it differently and all his other stale, old stories about being sick and getting help. Zoning him out I scanned the room for the prize I'd really been after, finding it sitting on the dresser by the window near his bed head. My trance was broken by the words "Are you ready," and the bad energy that followed as he stepped to towards me. "Wait!" "You have me in here, you're stronger than I am, surrender my passport as proof you'll keep your word". He turned towards the dresser, picked up the book, handed it slowly to me saying "I love you".

As soon as the book hit my hand and I could manage to take a few steps back I yelled for Jen who should have been right by the door waiting for her call. "I have it Jen, I have it!" But as usual, no Jennifer showed up. Instead I could hear her feet, lightly pounding across the tiles heading in our direction, and so did he. He made a dash for the door, slamming it, and then removing the only skeleton key that could open it. I clutched tightly to my hope and vowed he'd had to come real good to get me to let go.

"Give it to me now!" but I just clenched even tighter, feeling disbelief that it really had gotten to this point. His first attempt to grab it failed, we got into a wrestle match over it, but naturally I was no match to him so he won.

I pleaded with him to stop the madness, to come to his senses and really look at what he was doing and who he was doing it to. "Just give up the book, take me to the airport, and leave. You don't even have to say goodbye". "See I'm dressed and ready to go, I won't be a problem to you anymore, and when you get the help that you need, then we could come back home to you". Walking past me as if I wasn't speaking or even in the room, he reached into the top dresser draw, pulling out what first appeared to be a gun.

I stood my ground, trying my best to seem unshaken as he held it pointed to me, threatening to take my life if I didn't do as he instructed.

Realizing my defiant attitude and unwillingness to play his little game, he forced my participation by throwing me to the bed flat out on my back.

My squirming and twisting trying to get away irritated him so badly; he put his hand to my belly button in a motion to shoot, and then squeezed the trigger, as I braced for the pain of a bullet, or worse yet, wondering if I was still alive. I realized there was a blade on the tip of what was a gun a few seconds ago, and it was about 1cm from my navel. Leaning over top of me he bragged that he'd taken the knife from an inmate, so it wouldn't trace back to him if he used it to gut me like a fish. As all of this took place, Jen and Keta were banging and kicking the door. Shouting loudly for him to come to his senses and open the door, but he simply carried on as if it were just another day, with another of his lovers.

He ripped the zipper on my pants open, moving the knife upwards slowly to my neck, promising that one stupid move would end me. All I could do was lay there in silence, not because he demanded it, but as a hopeful means of escaping my body while he did what he did. I had schemed and plotted my way, day in and day out trying to avoid this very moment, wishing so dearly that I could leave before he ever got physical with me, well consciously. You see, with all the taunting he carried on with, I had no memory, just stories of which I could choose to not put an image, but this, this was a whole different thing. Now the stories would come to life, once that memory was created there was no undoing it. While I laid there pleading and begging, "I'm your daughter, your twin practically, you made me. "Please don't do this; I'm begging you please not to. I'll have to live with this for the rest of my life if you do this" I begged and pleaded for him to come to his senses and take me to the airport, but he just kept on. He ripped my pants some more to free them from my clenched ass cheeks, pulling them down to my ankle, taking my drawers with them.

I was naked and exposed in front of my father. I fought back in hopes that he would use the knife and kill me, so long as that memory no longer had a chance to be created. He pulled his penis from his pants, yanked my ass to the edge of the bed, fell to his knees and placed his tongue inside of me. It wasn't until I managed to lift my head from the bed and look down at my father between my thighs that I realize all this was really happening. I closed my eyes in hopes of imagining myself somewhere else, but then a strange sound filled the room. I looked down to see him stroking his penis, with his tongue doing the same between my legs.

He placed two of his fingers inside of me, and my world ended. He'd stripped me of my innocence. Not my virginity, no, thank goodness not that, but everything it was that made me a child, pure and innocent. He broke in through doors for which he had no keys, tainting a life he was meant to protect.

My screams and scratches, begging and yelling, not even the pounding and kicking at the door deterred him from what he was set out to do, he simply kept on until he was fully gratified then casually picking himself up off the floor grabbing a towel to wipe himself clean. He threw one at me and motioned for me to follow suit, but I tossed it to the floor, trying to find the strength to pull up my underwear to my waist in an effort to hide my body from the shame and disgrace casted upon it. As I did he took the knife from the bed and ripped the sides of my panties, lifting it to his nose then taking a deep breath. "I'll keep this for after you're gone so I can remember you", he said as he turned and hid it in a drawer.

Covering my naked body with what was left of my pants I tried as best I could to stand to my feet, as they hit the floor, I spotted the passport on the dresser, he followed my eyes and landed there too, picking up that I was fixing to make a dash for it. He swung the knife towards me, and then swiftly dove after the book, grabbing and clutching it tightly, holding my freedom hostage once again. "Bitch where you think you going? We made an arrangement and you brazenly try to bring down shame pon me? All you had to do was just shut yuh rass mouth, and then all would be ok". "Well let me see how you going to get to merica now when I get finish with this."

I grabbed the waist of my ripped pants and hopped behind him as fast as I could. "Jennifer him going in the bathroom to mash up mi passport" I sobbed as loudly as I could tears rushing down my sweaty face. He hastened his footsteps, beating her there, running to turn the shower on. He opened to the page where my visa was, placed it under the shower, then rubbed with all his might to remove my picture, or at least to an unrecognizable point. By the time Jennifer got to the door he had already thrown it to the floor, stepped past me spitting on the floor by my feet then looked me in the eyes and callously said, "Bitch go merica now?

I fell to the floor, weeping, as I scooped my last bit of hope up from the floor, holding it tightly in my bosom, hoping that when I looked inside it would be better than I thought. He turned to look at all of us one last time and said, "Even if it still works, you have four hours until you flight, and I'm not taking you. How are you getting there?"

If I had me a gun I would have shot that man dead. "You got what you wanted from me", I yelled at him, "What more do you want, my soul?" He walked to his room and slammed the door shut in my face.

When I finally opened the book to assess the damage it was better than it looked. There was evidence of tampering and some water marks, but other than that you could see my little face. Luckily my ticket was in there as well, so if I even had to go to the main road, leaving everything behind, begging for a ride to the airport I was grateful for my hope.

Once I finally got the chance to jump in that tub I washed his nastiness off of me, scrubbing myself as if a new vagina would appear if I scrubbed hard enough. Never in a million years would I have fathomed all these things would happen to me. You hear folks talk, and you watch movies but never had I ever thought my father would be capable of such acts, yet here we were. Coming to the reality that no matter if I scrubbed for another hundred years it couldn't undo what happened. I got a grip of myself, reassessed the situation, dried my tears, and got dressed.

The fact was I had less than four hours to get to that airport, because that plane was leaving with or without us. While Jennifer tried her best to convince him to take us, I jumped the fence to beg Mr. Carlton to help us out, which he would have gladly done on any other day, but that day of all days as my lucky streak would have it, the van wasn't working, and his son was gone on a job with the other vehicle. I thought of just going down to the main street, jumping on one of the busses and simply tell the conductor the truth, and I knew I would have gotten there, but Jennifer stopped me as I grabbed my things, begging me to give her one last chance to redeem herself. I told her she had five minutes.

There was a huge "Ackee"; tree that sat in the back of the yard. That tree had built so many good memories, like when my mother would sit by the trunk cleaning the fresh fish my father brought in from sea, but that day, it would be a special place of prayer.

Those days were happy days, but now I found myself in the same place, alone, shattered, but still not broken. Despite all that happened and was still going on I tried to find one last little bit of hope to cling to. Most things they tried to teach me at church were never believable or taken seriously, but I knew there had to be some bigger energy of which I was a part, that somehow it had been sustaining me and helping me see clearly the next step to take. Paired with my will to live, I knew this energy would not have taken me that far, given me that great of a story to have me conquered that easily. Neither gender nor names were important in that moment, I prayed to whatever had kept me thus far. Whatever it was that kept giving me that gut feeling that it would be alright, even if that meant it was me and my will to survive.

Praying out loud I promised that if I made out of there alive, landed safely in the U.S, that I'd make sure one day I'd do something, say something, be something more to prevent another child, or a few more little Monique's from going through what I was going through, promised that I'd do good, and be good, remain humble, and somehow find a way to live a happy normal life. At that moment I didn't see how that would be possible, but I promised. I promised to help make it easier to speak without fear of backlash from "inside" sources failing to uphold their responsibilities. I looked to the heavens, the only place I knew at the time god existed, dried my tears, while proclaiming loudly with all the sureness I could summon, "I'm leaving this island today, by the hook or the crook!" Using the tree trunk to lift off the ground, I dusted the dirt from my butt, and rose to my feet.

Just as her time was about to expire, Jennifer came shouting for me to get my things and get in the van. Something she said while trying to persuade him triggered his sympathy I suppose or maybe he finally realized what would happen if I stayed, as it was no longer a secret, everyone knew. Whatever the reason he changed his mind. I jumped for joy hauling ass to get my things. It was as if I'd signed a bond with the words I'd spoken, and perhaps the truth in my words helped, whatever the reason I vowed to keep my word.

He refused to help me with my luggage and instructed me to sit in the back, which was just fine with me. I didn't care if I had to ride on the hood of that car; I was getting off the island one way or another. We waved good bye to the neighbors as we left the driveway, though I had felt so much anger towards them for never trying to do more, I understood that they shouldn't and wouldn't have had to do more if my father behaved as a responsible parent would have. Looking back at the house I said my goodbye's to a place of horror, grateful to never having to grace its halls ever again.

When we arrived at the airport, he didn't even attempt to get out of the vehicle in any kind of way to help me. He knew I wouldn't say a word; knowing that I'd much rather let him go and get away, than to rat and risk them keeping us there, so he spared me the usual shut my mouth speech. Bags unloaded, I didn't even turn to him to say goodbye, I allowed my sister to say good bye told Jennifer thanks for helping to get us there, then scooted away, fast and in a hurry. I walked as fast as I could without running, in fear he would change his mind, jump from the van, grab me, then driving off with me. I wasn't taking any chances.

Back then the airport was so small that glass was the only thing between you and your loved ones and the immigration officers. Needless to say he could see everything as it took place between me and the officer, keeping in mind my passport was soaking wet. Just as expected the first question they asked was, "Why is this book soaking wet?" I turned my head to my left looking out the glass, staring at the devil that taunted and tainted me for almost three years. In that quick of a second the entire ordeal flashed through my mind, and I thought of all the options and which would be best. Sure I could have snitched on that old pervert, and though it would only bring a wonderful momentary satisfaction, it would not necessarily have the best long run benefits. I thought quickly to lose the moment and win another day. Giving her my attention once more, I told her that my sister in the states had sent me some money to have as pocket change, since my younger sister and I were traveling alone. I told her that it had been raining the day before, as I was going to the western union to collect the money she'd sent. She didn't buy it at first, either due to the fact that I wasn't yet 18, or because she followed my eyes to my father, and felt the chill I did from staring in his eyes. When our eyes met again it's as if she'd seen everything. She handed me my passport, leaned in, smiled, and said;" You take care and enjoy your trip". She didn't have to say another word, only we could ever testify to, or truly understand that moment.

With hope and time, I knew I was fixable. There were many battle scars, some I knew would take a lot of tears to heal, but nothing was broken. Sure my trust would be gone for some time, but even at that tender age, I realized that it could have been so much worse than it was, and giving up would only give him the right to say he won.

We landed in Fort Lauderdale instead of Philly, as my sister was receiving us, she was very pregnant and about to pop, so traveling up north was out of the question. As the air hostess handed us over, I ran to hug my mother as quickly as I could, like a receipt I guess that I had really made it out alive.

This sister was new to me as we had different fathers and grew up without knowing the other existed until I was about 12. Though no shame on my part, as I was ready to yell my story from the mountain tops, I remembered the sweeping it under the rug speech, and thought it best to contain my tongue until the timing was right. For the moment I basked in the glory that I had gotten away.

Once we arrived and settled in at the house I dragged my mother outside so I could bring her up to date with the day's showdown. She told me that the most important thing was our safety no longer being threatened, that any justice due to him would be taken care of later, for the moment all we could do was try our best to act like it didn't happen.

Her words soothed me, yet caused so much confusion and pain all over again. Was she going to be satisfied with the fact that we were there with her? Would that be enough for her to just forget it all and not seek correction on my behalf? Only time would tell that tale, for the moment, being in a safe and warm bed was enough for me. We spent the next few days looking towards Christmas presents and getting to know our new sister, niece and nephew, it was truly a happy time.

A little after Christmas my sister went into labor, and right in the nick of time, as we were scheduled for a train to Philly that day, barely having enough time to stop by the hospital to say our goodbyes and meet the twins.

I left Florida a new person. Unsure of the future, but knowing that if I had survived my father, there was no obstacle that I could not overcome and get back up from. I gave thanks for the fact that my mother had sense enough to get me away from him whether she would help me tell my story or not.

9

I suppose this is the chapter that you've been looking forward to the entire time. The chapter where I tell you that we arrived in Philadelphia safely, everything worked out merrily and we lived happily ever after. That mom tried her hardest to make sure what was left of my childhood was preserved, and she showed me the love I would so dearly need to put my life back in or and make some sense of it all. Well I can tell you that, and it would all be true. She got us into school, we went to church almost every day as usual and above all I was safe when I slept at night. But it only lasted for about a year.

My mother worked day in and day out, practically living on the job, leaving me the oldest in charge, expecting me to behave as if I understood the ropes, and having enough sense to keep things leveled as she tried her best to make the situation work. It was sort of me helping her to help me kind of thing, and I could respect that fully. Finally after being an illegal immigrant for a little under ten years, not being able to travel home, having to run through loops and circles to get by, her green card was approved. Once that card hit the door, she was on a flight out of the country as soon as she could pack.

When she left everything was pretty normal. I held it down, and took care of home while she was away. After all I was happy for my mother, knowing the torment myself of seeing people come and go, while you could not. Although she hadn't cut things off completely with my father, they weren't close enough for me to think of him as a threat, I figured naturally she'd avoid any contact with him believing her to be somewhat normal, thus being turned off by the thought of sleeping with him. I wasn't even close to being ready for what was about to manifest in my life all over again.

Lying up in her lap as she played in my hair, like she had done so many times before, we talked and laughed, reminiscing of sweet ole Jamaica. She shared memories from her trip with me, and told me all the hellos that were sent to us from so many lips to her ears. Everything appeared to be going so well, when all of a sudden somehow my father's name came up, changing the atmosphere in the room. My hair was no longer being stroked, and sensing the seriousness of the mood; I sat up to see if I could get a conformation from her face. "Monique did your father really molest you?" "YES!" Instantly, without even the slightest hesitation I threw my answer back at her in a how dare you even ask me that tone of voice? Barely coming to grip with the reality that she'd actually asked me that question to begin with, she asked again. "Monique are you sure that you dad put his hands on you?" "Mommy I have no reason to lie, besides Keta and Jen were there, you know this, why now?" She caught me up to speed on the part of her trip she spent with my father, during which he told her that I was a lying little shit. According to her, he said he may have accidentally touched me inappropriately, even groped me, but that he stopped once Jennifer confronted him. She even reported that he said I was the one being fresh, forcing myself on him. I froze solid on the spot.

This was not happening. I really had no intention in signing up for this all over again. Staring in her eyes, hoping that maternal love would cause her to have something in that place where I had seen darkness in my father. As if truly his twin flame, she also lacked any ray of light or hope. "I'm your daughter! Are you really going to believe a man before you believe me?" The next thing I knew the broom stick was all over my body. With each stroke I had multitasked, breathing, dodging, and asking why the hell she was beating me, what it was I had done? Finally satisfied after getting in a few good hits she told me the beating was for having no manners. Having no manners? "But he did molest me! You shouldn't even question if I'm being truthful or not, the fact that something like this can be coming out my mouth must mean that something had to have provoked those thoughts". "Besides, what reason would I have to want to tell lies on my father, didn't he practically give us everything we asked? But anyone who knows my mother knows that she is what you would call "dark" or arrogant and ignorant. Combine that with the voodooed love potion obsession she had for my father and you'd had every reason for her to ignore all I was saying and stick to my father's story.

She resumed her torture, yelling that I was trying to come between her and her husband. I cried, not because of the pain from the beating, but more so because of the words coming from her mouth. Speaking my mind I revealed that I thought them both unfit parents, but from her I expected a maternal bond. I told her had it been my child I'd believe them, even without needing evidence to prove them right or wrong. She heaped all the clothes she found that belonged to me, threw them in some bags, tossed them outside, and then told me my black butt had to go. Luckily her best friend "Sis Grace" knew about most of what happened, and decided to take me in while my mother got her loose mental screws tightened.

Ms. Grace gave me the home I didn't have before, and in many ways I was happy it was all playing out the way it was. Truth is, put both my parents together and they didn't make a whole, so though my mother gave me a place to live, she really didn't understand what it meant to be a mom. Ms. Grace, showed compassion when I fucked up, my mom bitched if I cleaned the house from top to bottom and missed a spot. Her belief of being a good parent was having a job and seeing to it that we had full bellies. In that she did the best she could do, but where love was concerned the few times we had heard it was before daddy dearest went all wacko on us. Though she was busy and had a child of her own to raise, she always made the time to ask how my day was or if there was anything I needed. This was exactly the environment I needed, I was happy.

As if my mother just could not stomach the thought of me, the wretched one that stole her happy life and marriage from her, she just wouldn't ease up on making sure I was as miserable as she was. She called the house day and night, antagonizing and perplexing the woman to send me home. Ms. Grace tried her best to convince her that the same thing would happen again if I was to go back, but she insisted I was to come home. Not being my legal guardian put her back against the wall, and the nagging only made it worse, so Ms. Grace gave in and sent me home, reminding me that her door was always open to me.

Back in the unstable nest my mother forced me to call home, nothing much had really changed, nor was there any hope of it ever happening. We rarely ever spoke, brushed past each other in the hallways; hell the tension was so high the blind wouldn't miss it.

On my part I tried as best as I could to stay in line, while she tried to play the mother dearest role for the spectators. Having a live in job during the week and a weekend job every now and then gave us a lot of time apart, which made it that much easier for us to not kill each other, and avoid many arguments.

Any day she was home we fought and argued. Having the intelligence of about a 6th grader, she hated when I would drop a few intellectual sentences on purpose knowing she wouldn't understand. As punishment for making too much sense as to why they were horrible people, she would yell at me that I was just jealous that her husband wanted her and not me, that no matter what I did they'd never be apart. She'd tell me that she was sorry that I was born; that maybe if she had squeezed my head as I came from her she would have saved everyone a lot of trouble. That everything that happened to me was my fault, and I provoked it all. She told me that I was ugly, and no decent man in his right mind would want me. She even went as far as telling some family members and folks outside of the family the same lie. A few of my aunts and uncles cut her off for her neglect, telling her how much she had wronged me. Still she chose him, and each time we got into it she made it her duty to rape me all over again.

When I would tell her that it was the worst thing imaginable, those things she tells me, that her words are like the fingers that keep picking away at a scab, hindering that wound from ever healing, it did nothing to change her actions.

Enough! Needing that wound to heal so badly, and losing everything in me it took to not do something drastically irreversible, I decided he had to be outed. Obviously she had to be in a room full of witnesses, hearing the confession from his lips to her ears, for her to finally step out the bubble she was living in. Since she couldn't shut her trap long enough to keep peace with me for more than five minutes, and my cousin Alma was staying with us from Canada, I figured I'd use her to witness his confession, then maybe, just maybe , she'd listen to me then.

I scratched the silver dust from the calling card, dialed the number, entered my pin, then waited for him to pick up the phone;

my entire body was shaking from nervousness of it not working, and the anxiety of actually having him on record.

We made small talk so I could get him comfortable, managing to laugh just enough to convince him we were actually good. "Daddy why did you have oral sex with me, mess with me, and told my mom I forced myself onto you?" After a long pause he opened his mouth to the same man I'd left in Jamaica, insincere and full of shit. He softened his voice as he always did, then began his charade of, oh Mon I'm so sorry. "I know I've messed up your life and I know things will never be the same. I don't know why I did what I did but I'm sorry. It wasn't me; it's the voices in my head, the black man with the head wrap took over my head and made me do it".

I couldn't believe this excuse for a human being was really trying to bring the science of "obeah" (voodoo) into his pathetic reasons for his vile and disturbing actions. He was truly a narcissist, void of any true or genuine emotion, and he fell right into my trap of proving that to someone else that seemed somewhat coherent.

As soon as my mother walked into the house, barely having time to put her things down, I rushed towards her, yelling that I had proof that I wasn't lying. She turned to my cousin looking confused, only to have her confirm that everything I had told her about my father was indeed true. Not surprising she wasn't jumping for joy or ecstatic about the truth; actually she looked as if she could kill me for doing what I did. She needed so badly to believe I was lying, asking my cousin every question in the book about how I got the information out of him a question to which my cousin replied asking if any of that really mattered now that she had proof it all happened. Finally deciding to accept my cousin's word as truth she came to some sight that it was all true, she fell to her knees, leaned in on the bed and wept. She ordered me to run to the 7 Eleven on the corner to get her a card so she could hear him confess with her own ears.

He answered the phone as if he was expecting her to do exactly as she was doing, and had no problem repeating everything he'd said to us earlier that afternoon. You would think that would have been my golden ticket, if not for the love I so craved and needed, at least the stopping of the beatings, slandering and lies in my name.

She played cool for about a year and things were somewhat normal. We spoke a bit more, even sharing an occasional laugh or two, but if you had sense enough, you'd see right through the façade of it all. All her actions towards me showed that she merely kept the peace because outsiders somewhat believed me.

Whenever it was back to school time, she'd give me $100 dollars to get everything I needed for the rest of the year. One uniform pant alone was about $20. My winter jacket was an old navy blue windbreaker, with a rip by the pocket, she'd gotten from her patients son. New to the cold that was the most brutal breaking in of the cold weather one could ever imagine, and the worst part was she wore a mink jacket to church on Sundays, with and equally ugly old

British style church suit that cost anywhere from $200-400. She even sent money to my father in Jamaica whenever he needed, while barely giving me money to get through the week. I guess to her, she did her duty as long as there was food in the house when I got home. I felt so much disdain for her, because it was bad enough he did what he did, but here she was condoning him, in the same suit treating me as if I had done something to deserve all of this.

Always remembering what that math teacher taught me all those years back, I managed to make it through, always rapping with folks I met treating people right, keeping the good heart I had, I made friends in high places, so I always somehow ended up ok.

After a year of what we called peace, she snapped like a twig one day. Somehow we got into an argument, and the gates of hell burst wide open. She let everything out she'd been holding the entire time, putting some licks on me, like I was starring a slavery movie. Needless to say she made it very clear who she favored, and it sure af wasn't me.

This put me in a zero fucks given state. I didn't care what happened to me anymore. Here I was trying my best to please the one person that cared the least about me. I busted my ass making exceptional grades in school, and I can't even remember her once caring enough to say she was proud. I'd had about all I could take, ran out of rope, and I was about ready to let it show. I started smoking weed, hanging out with older boys, and played hooky from school. I lost value for myself, feeling as though if my father didn't protect it and mother neglected it, then hell I sure as hell could abuse it. With her providing minimally for me financially, being legally unable to work, I learned how the older girls, the ones that truly played the guys, taking their shit, without giving back operated, studying them and perfecting their moves. It was such a power play for me, something I had lost a ways back.

I began dating one of those older guys eventually for some time, keeping it as secret as I could, but my nosey, annoying, loud ass uncle happened to be staying with us at the time. Not only was he all up in everyone's business, he sometimes messed with that "white lady" and when he did his mouth became a loose cannon, repeating anything his eyes saw. I'd always respected my mother's crib, and just tried overall to avoid people being all up in my business. She went to Jamaica, and some part of me wanted to exact revenge on her if even silently for treating me as badly as she had, so I decided to desecrate her couch with my fluids, and so I did, unaware my uncle was downstairs.

My mother hadn't put her bags down for more than an hour before my uncle came running from the basement, shouting out his dry, ashy lips, that all I did while she was gone was sex out her couch. "All I could hear was boing, boing, boing all weekend!" "Fucking cokehead", I thought to myself, as I turned to my mother, trying my best to appear as if I cared a bit, all the while laughing inside. To be honest I really didn't expect her to get upset, after all she thought it was ok when my father did it to me, so it had to be absolutely ok for me to do as I pleased with myself right? But nope she cared a whole lot. After all seeing me miserable had become her new journey in life. She called the cops, made a big deal, called everyone and created as much excitement as she could over the whole ordeal. She saw to it that everyone saw that indeed I was a bad little whore, and they believed.

This bothered me for weeks. Keep my father a secret, but disgrace me when I choose? It was time to stop holding the family secret. It was time to unleash all that happened, time for everyone to see who the true monster was. I rained the same terror upon her that she'd released upon me for so many years, airing all her dirty laundry , revealing to everyone we knew, all those people who thought I actually forced myself onto my father, never stopping for a second to ask even if I did, could that ever justify him accepting such an offer? In the process I learned the more I released and revealed, the better I felt. I told him, her and the old lady, no one was off limits.

Feeling disgraced, and never expecting me to open my mouth, in fear she would take what little she was providing away, she told everyone I was laying on her husband, that I made the whole thing up to come between them. Just as they did back home, with the exception of a very few, they all whispered, but none came to ask me about it.

Of course the beatings resumed, and got worse each time someone else came to her to question whether or not she really did the things they had heard she did. The only hope I felt was Mon-Fri while she was at work, giving me time to hang with the dough boys, learning the codes in the streets, and most of all how to survive. Sex was fun, but I realized that survival was going to be the most valuable asset for the storm that was about to hail on my life. The facts were I had no papers and my mother was on the verge of putting me out.

And just as soon as my most necessary lessons were learnt, the levies broke and hell went flooding over. My breaking point had come. I'd grown tired of the beatings and being unable to bring myself to slapping her senseless. I'd come to the reality that none of it was my fault, understanding just how much both parent were at fault, one way or another.

The worst and last day of the beatings, she came home as usual with frustration therapy on her mind, but this day she went so far, my cousin Norma living upstairs had to run to my rescue. When she finally decided to stop, the broom stick and I were equally bruised. My cousin had heard the fights before, but this day I decided to fight back. I had survived too much to come settle for another life of hell.

Not being able to fight back with my fists, I used my voice, yelling between the hits that I'd had enough, and that I just might have her locked up. Those who know my mother well enough will testify her one true greatest fear after drowning is the law. Her name has never even been to the credit bureau's office before! Knowing that my calling would put her in a whole lot of trouble she asked Ms. Grace to take me in once more, promising to leave me be. She told me I was never allowed to step foot in her house ever again, and that was just fine by me.

Playing hooky made it impossible to pass my classes, and my attendance records showed me absent more than I was present, so naturally they requested for my mother to come in for a meeting. There everyone learnt just how badly my grades had slipped and how awful my behavior was, although not the worst kid, always remaining polite, I was fucking up where my future was concerned, but no one saw it as a cry for attention, or help, no one in that room thought anything of me but me being a bad seed. I was ordered to have all my teachers sign a sheet of paper before and after class every day. No one in that meeting saw anything odd, but now under the close surveillance of any and every authority, and in my 11th grade year of school my guidance counselor found something odd while looking over my files, causing her to summon me to her office. Walking into that meeting that day I had no idea that my guidance counselor at Roxborough High School, Mrs. Wilson, would forever impact and change my life.

Hesitating at first to open up to her, she insisted that something had to be dreadfully wrong somewhere for me to be acting out like this. The more I tried to tell her I wasn't acting, that it was all me, the more proof she showed to prove otherwise. She pointed out that I had been getting straight A's up until the middle of the 10th grade right before I got transferred from my old school Martin Luther King H.S for protection from a fight involving some American kids who didn't take likely to anyone outside their culture. She said she'd even spoken with all my teachers who agreed that my polite behavior was a contradiction to the way I tried to be rude on purpose. They all agreed that I was trying to be something I was not. All of this evidence caused her to ask, why, and what happencd?

At long last someone in a position of authority finally asked the one question it took for me to free my heart and mind of the burden it so desperately sought to let go of. She knew the entire story from beginning to end in about 45 mins, well the shortest version to the point.

With her mouth still opened in shock she grabbed the receiver of the office phone, ready to call the proper authorities, but I managed to stop her before she could finish dialing. As quickly as I could, I explained to her that making that call would not be beneficial, as I was already out of my mother's house, living in a very safe environment. Had she finished that call, my sister and I would end up wards of the state, and although exacting revenge would have been just and fair, I had to also think of my sister. She was an innocent party in all of this, and although the chips were stacked against me with my mother, she seemed to care enough to ensure that little sis was properly taken care of.

Placing the receiver on the base she looked up into my eyes, piercing my soul on purpose, and then uttered the single most important speech of my early adult life. "I get that you are angry, that your parents don't care, so you think it's ok if you don't care too. I know you feel it doesn't matter what happens to you, or if you even have a future. But remember your mother is old, and from the sounds of it very bitter, and not about to change anytime soon." "Her chance at change is gone. She's going to be doing the same thing, working the same job, living in the same denial until she dies. Your father, he will reap what he has sewn one day, if not justice for you, by some other means." "You, you are young and full of potential and possibility. Why waste your time being bitter, when you can be better? They expect you to fail, so prove them wrong! None of this is your fault!"

I smiled, a real, true, happy smile, sighed a deep new breath, and for the first time in a long time, I had a renewed will to really live. She presented me with two paths, one would end in my certain failure, the other would take hard work, making up classes at odd hours of the morning, but it would lead to a road that held so much potential. My future now rested in my hands, wherever it went from that moment was all on me, so I accepted the latter. She became a hero to me that day, and just as I had gotten myself into that hole, I'd use her words to help me get myself out.

Working off the books and being illegal was the worst and most cheated experience ever. Mohammed, the owner of a pizza house, knew he was doing me a favor, and took advantage by paying me 90 bucks per week, after coming in Mon-Fri, 6pm-1am, because he knew he was helping me out by paying me cash, he knew just how much overboard he went on my cut. Nevertheless, I was thankful that I could help myself out, not wanting to be a burden on anyone. Even though Ms. Grace never let me feel that way, it was the least I could do to help out, her being a trying single mom herself. I had turned things around so much at school with my grades, being present and punctual, and just my overall turn around landed me in good favor with my superiors. They allowed me to leave school at 12, granted I understood that it was my responsibility that all my work was turned in.

My new attitude was definitely working in my best interest, and the timing couldn't have been more perfect, with things running as smoothly as they were 12th grade came and was nearing it's ending in no time. I can still remember running to lock myself in a bathroom stall to bawl my eyes out after a homeroom session. We'd been discussing prom that morning, and somewhere in the rules and regulations list, I lost myself. The reality that there had been so many paths, that I had survived, being unsure of what was ahead, but ever so glad that in that moment, being able to pay for my own everything, man that was an overwhelming feeling. I was so jealous when I heard the other kids bragging about family members seeing them off, having block parties, and getting money pinned on them, knowing the two people I had were my best friends Brian and Alisha. Being thankful for wonderful friends, I tagged along without even feeling like the third wheel, their family even pinned a dollar or two on me as well, and I went to my prom feeling like a million bucks, because I had beaten the odds.

Next up was graduation, which by no means was easily attained, but so very deserving. My journey being the one it was had to throw me a curve ball. My aunt, who was on her way in from New York, went into active labor, forcing her to rush to the hospital, and all the hope riding on my cousin Trudy also from the Big Apple, went through the window when she got lost in Allentown Pa, which left my little sister stuck in the house waiting to be picked up by her

My silver lining came when I realized that, I had done the hard work, I had come this far, and all that mattered was that I was there to represent myself. Luckily, my cousin Stacy, made it just in the nick of time, as I sashayed, across the stage, satisfied in my accomplishments. The next day I was on a bus with all my belongings on my way to NY to take care of my aunt's new baby girl, while she was at work.

This was my chance to have a new start, one that I owned.

10

Making a little money while helping Aunt Marcia was satisfying, she was really mellow, but she had her days, one thing for sure, she loved me, always had since I was a little girl, even when everyone else favored my sister. While being able to help her was a pleasure, my eighteenth birthday had just passed and I wanted to see the world. I was ready to create my own memories for the rest of my life. My aunt and I having the relationship we had, being all protective of me as her own feared my leaving, but understood fully, and gave me her blessings.

Having no legal papers, made finding that new life just a bit harder than I had imagined it would be. Through resilience, determination and the will to live I walked through eight feet of snow to the first real job of my life.

It was a popular Jamaican reggae station in the Bronx, and as it so happened they needed an office assistant, and I had the perfect lie. Computer skills I'd picked up along the way would be quite sufficient, but he was looking for an intern to fill the position. He took me on nonetheless, as he was impressed by my determination, walking through the snow and all. Hey, becoming a child of the streets wakes you up to the reality that you'd better be quick on your feet.

I rented a single bedroom in a boarding house off White Plains road, in the Bronx. I was getting paid, buying my own groceries, taking care of myself, and doing so well might I add. I'd come so far, from the battered little girl that left Jamaica a few years ago. There'd been so much visible growth, but still I had so much anger and bitterness that consumed me on the inside. At nights I'd lay in my room, staring up at the ceiling, thinking of the many ways I was going to exact my revenge upon them both. During the day I wore a smile that masked the pain, keeping it hidden, buried deep.

I suppose when people don't know your story, they don't show much compassion, and as I said having no papers in this country, makes a bad situation, even worse. My boss took full advantage of this fact, aware that he was doing me a favor by paying cash; he suggested I return the favor in the bed. My refusal to comply resulted in my pay being a couple days late every week, messing up my payments with my landlady. Making things worse he asked me to complete tasks he knew I wasn't capable of, forcing me into a corner to either quit, or be fired. Life on my own was no easy road indeed, but I chose it, nothing was forced on me, I could truly live, instead of simply existing.

Lying in my bed one hot summer night, hiding from my landlord, I thought of olden days, and how far I gotten through the power of the will to live. Something or someone had my back, but I wasn't wrapped up in worries of just what, I followed my gut to leave New York, trusting that I'd be just fine.

Friday nights I was entrusted to collect the money from the door, at a party my boss hosted weekly. Every night I worked, I gave him every honest dollar that came into my hand, never biting the hand that fed. Now he had pushed my back against the wall, and with no other vision of getting out, I plotted to take half the door that week.

Holding the most money I'd ever held in my entire life, I called my sister down south to let her know I'd be there in a few days, bought a suitcase, told my boss to kick rocks, and after paying my landlady what I owed for rent, I said my goodbyes to the city that never sleeps.

I tried to be on my best behavior, as a token of appreciation to my sister for taking me in. She was my second eldest sister, the second for my mother, older than me by only seven years, raising her two children and making a life of her own, the less worries she had about me the better, but I was a misguided child, with no leash and all the perks of being a free eighteen years old, with neither chick nor child to care for. All that hope of being good went through the door hanging with my sister's husband one afternoon. Running some errands we ran into one of his best friends, who just happened to be my past school mate from Shortwood Primary. We were not acquainted then, just passed each other in the corridors, as he was a couple years older than me.

We clicked while playing catch up, exchanged numbers, which led to us hanging out just about every day, and with just a bit of too much free time on my hands, trouble came looking and I went answering. In no time I swore I was in love, he was everything I thought I needed to survive. We became really close friends, and in a short time, added benefits. Believing all the lies planted in my head, and having little to no self-worth, I disregarded the fact the he lived with his girl, even getting reckless enough to go unprotected, which led to my first real scare, missing my period for a week.

Never having proper guidance or teachings about such matters, I carried on not fully understanding what could possibly be at stake. All the ladies the men from his crew of three, hung out together, and since I was now with him, if even only on the side, I was initiated in the group too. I chose the two that were in my shoe. They were just as illegal as I was, smoked as much weed, and partied just as I liked. One thing we didn't have in common though was that they took care of themselves by "buttering" clothes from stores for resale. Their favorite store was Vicky's, and that's where my first lesson took place. They introduced me to a world for which I seemed to have a natural knack, upping my game to stealing champagne from pharmacies. I loved the thrill of it all, but mostly that I didn't have to ask a soul for a thing.

Having more experience than I did, with just under 10 kids between them all, they suggested that I took a pregnancy test, thinking that I may have been pregnant, due to my always feeling nauseated. I bought one of those cheap generic brands, illiterate to the importance of timing, and procedures. The test came back negative; I breathed my sigh of relief, grateful for the results, and then carried on, unshaken by what had happen. I was so out of control, lost, and I had just the right company to take me further down that path. My sister tried her best to warn me that no good would come from me hanging with that crowd of girls, I refused to listen, and she was too busy taking care of home to play parent with me.

Sure enough karma caught up with me. Stuffing our girdles full with thousands of dollars' worth of undies I got a gut feeling to just walk away and leave it all, I tried convincing my partners in crime, but they weren't having it.

Neglecting what I felt I followed them on in a high end clothing store I knew I should have stayed clear of. As we stuffed our outfits to go out that night, I began to wonder why it was so effortless, why no one even suspected us. As I looked up, I saw a gay guy smiling his ass off, trying his hardest not to look my way, and something deep down just kept nagging for me to walk away. But I wanted to be cool, so I ignored once again.

Walking to the car we laughed and cheered about the huge score we had all made, and how easy it was. No sooner than we got to the car, and I grabbed the handle, a hand was around my neck. The cops got us, recovered the goods, charged us with grand theft and left me for the night.

I cried like a baby, snot and all running down my face. I had bumped my toe real hard, and I had done it all by myself. A few weeks later, the charges were dropped, and so was I, right in West Palm Beach, back to my eldest sister, where I had begun this journey all those years ago.

I was determined not to mess up, to change, be better, and live up to the promise I made myself in Mrs. Wilson's office, but I was consumed by so much anger and hate. All I wanted was a simple apology from the both of them. I knew it wouldn't change the past, but it could sure make the future look possible. So with no one to talk to about my inner demons, I lashed out on myself.

Sleep was rare, not wanting to face the demons of my dreams; I partied every night of the week, smoking, drinking, and living in bliss, even if superficial. The only medicine that seemed to totally numb the pain was sex, a habit easily satisfied when living in the party scene. Making the matter worse, I didn't enjoy having sex as it would take me to a very dark place in time and memory, but it was the only remedy for the lack of love I felt, a false promise, that perhaps if given that love would be satisfied. I never allowed myself to be silent with my thoughts for very long, not even in my dreams, often jumping from nightmares, covered in cold sweat.

I fought so hard to stay away from those horrid memories, forbidding myself from ever returning to that dark place.

Of course once the memory is created there is only so much you can truly do to escape them indefinitely, and unable to control them I saw one way to make them go away permanently. Kill myself! After all, I thought no one really cared; no one would miss my presence. Hell, I began to stop giving a fuck about me! I bought ten packs of those single serve Tylenols PM's, with two in each, confident that would suffice in getting the job done. After emptying all the pills in my mouth, found a comfortable spot in the couch and prepared to enter the light.

When my eyes next opened, I had no idea how long my I'd been out for, but I woke up to my sister yelling, I couldn't die in her care. She bought me a one way ticket back to NY, since I convinced a friend of mine to let me stay until I got on my feet.

Another toss off, another person that just didn't have the time for my problems, but I understood, thankful that she had even taken me in, gave her one last hug as I got ready for another path on my journey. As I left her grasp, she asked me a most peculiar question for the moment, wanting to know how come I hadn't had my cycle that month. I brushed it off, telling her my body was probably switching up, and there was nothing to worry about, because that was truly what I believed to be true.

I had twenty two hours of silence ahead of me to truly reflect and make some changes.

11

As if destiny needed me to return to Philly, my stay in NY got cut really short after I began getting so sick I couldn't even keep water down. Undocumented, and in fear that the stories I'd been told of homeland security on the lookout for illegal immigrants, there was only one clinic I knew to seek treatment. Luckily my friend Kayon, from Sunday school days looked out, giving me a place to crash. She tried to convince me that I was pregnant because of the symptoms I was having, but I refused to believe that could be. I needed to believe that it wasn't so, as bumming it out on someone's couch was cool if you were traveling solo.

You're pregnant! Words that would forever change my life, but in that moment I couldn't understand it as such, the furthest my thoughts could reach, was how unable and difficult it would be to raise that child in the situation I was in. Young, scared and impulsive, the first words out of my mouth were to ask how long before I could get rid of it. I wasn't ready to take the risk of bringing a child into the world I was living in, I didn't think it fair. How would I feed it being undocumented, and what if it was a girl how would I guarantee she would the same fate I did?

The doc told me she had to check it's heartbeat just to make sure everything was ok, and as I listened I wondered if she had been seasoned in the knowledge of what connection that created, and with that I knew there was no going back, that this would be my chance to do things differently. I thought maybe this child could be the bridge in mending the relationship with my own mother, and after further encouragement from Ms. Grace, I decided to have my baby.

Needing someplace to stay, and not thinking my mother to be so vile as to leave me homeless, I returned to a place I thought for certain would remain in my past. At first she hesitated to let me stay with her, but for the sake of her grandchild I suppose, she allowed it. There were good days, bad days, and just horribly awful days. On the latter we would argue so loudly, my cousin Tasha, who lived in the downstairs apartment, would have to run up the stairs to quell things before they escalated to any physical contact. Tasha was also my sanity, without her I was sure that baby would not make it alive outside of my body, or I would have probably attempted to take my mother's life. Out of spite and wanting to embarrass my mother, I used her ignorance and lack of education against her to win the argument, spitting something with enough depth or saying some fancy word I knew she wouldn't get, so I could watch the smirk on Tash's face over my victory. My mother's comeback would always try to hurt me equally by telling me that everything was my fault, and I deserved every bit of it, that I was just bitter because her husband wanted her and not me.

I felt so sorry for her; she was such a sad case. Any woman that could still find it possible to become stimulated by a man who forced himself on a child, let alone her own, even if she merely suspected it could have happened, had to be a pretty sad case. It cut so deeply whenever she spoke her thoughtless words, but I knew I needed her to help make sure this baby had at the very least shelter over its head.

My mother's love for those hideous church suits caused her to work two, sometimes three jobs, but that was just fine with me. My sister, a little more grown and mature, was in her last year of high school, which meant I was home with my cousin and best friend all day, she was even the closest thing I'd have in place of the baby's father.

Remember that cheap test I did, well I'd assumed all was well and fell out of touch with the young man, and my sister's split with her hubby meant I had no way to get in touch. Tasha was my rock, and there for me for everything, understanding my pain at the time, being in the same boat herself. She was even the only one there when I learnt I was bringing a little girl into the world and snot nosed cried all the way home on the subway. I'd so dreamt of having a boy; because I thought he'd stand a better chance at surviving this very cold world. That day to comfort me, she hugged me and my big ole belly, reminding me that I wasn't a boy, but I was tougher than nails.

Those words of advice and revelation of truth would come to be tested not long after they were uttered. Seven months pregnant as round as a bowling ball, so close to the end and so not the time for the drama, I overheard my mother on the phone with my father, giving him permission to come and stay with us for a couple weeks. She didn't know I was aware of her little scheme, so when I headed to my cousins Trudy's house up in Connecticut, she had no reason to be suspicious of my actions.

My cousin and I sat in her kitchen in disbelief of just how horrible the actions of my mother were, as I gave her all the details up to the current moment. Her actions were simply too hard to accept. Why would she, how could she? I would not step foot inside that house, so long as that beast was breathing inside of it. I just wasn't ready to face that monster yet.

Two weeks into my trip my mother called, demanding that I came home. I begged and pleaded with her, telling her how frightened I was of him, not wanting to be alone in the house with him at any time. She threatened that if I wasn't in that house before my father left, then I'd better not come back at all. When I asked why it mattered that I be there before he left, without any empathy at all, she said, "Your father wants to see you", and so with no long term hope of surviving without her help, remembering that she was also filing my residency paperwork, I left Connecticut. That trip all I did was cry, remembering how far I'd come, although filled with anger, I knew I had to keep it together for the sake of the unborn life inside me.

Whenever my father tried to hug me I pushed him away, reminding him that I wasn't a child and didn't have to do a damn thing he said, my mother insisted that I kept my manners in check, and remain respectful, but I was a grown woman, and besides, I dared either one of them to try and make me respect an incestuous pedophile.

On the inside I was so scared for me and my baby, but I knew I had more power now, I was 19 years old, not some scared 11 year old baby, I'd really hurt this dude if he tried me then called the cops. In fact a little part of me wanted his stupid ass to try his fuckery in this country. Still I was human, and some fear lingered with him being there, so I took the extra precaution of wearing three pairs of pajamas, just as when I was a kid. I programmed myself to sleep during the day when Tasha was home, and stayed up all night, doing whatever it took to stay safe.

I never knew such hate could exist, as the one I felt towards my mother for what she had put me through. I wasn't asking her not to live out her sick fantasy and have her dream man, I was simply asking to be excused when she needed her fix. But that was the problem, I was his fix, and she'd fix his fix, long as it fixed her fix.

Thanksgiving couldn't come fast enough. I needed him to leave ASAP, but at the very least I could appreciate that everything so far was going in my favor. He kept his distance and hung out in the living room at nights, and respected my space and unwillingness to interact with him on any level.

Thanksgiving Day 04, a day that went down in the history book of my life. Before we could finish eating breakfast, the doorbell started going off and the house slowly started to fill with family and friends from near and far, who all came to eat and mingle. I said my hello's, made small talk, answered a few nosy family members' questions, and then slid off to get some sleep on the couch under the A/C, trying to escape the heat from the kitchen, and make up for the sleep I'd lost the previous night.

When I woke up, about midday, to a house now even louder and more crowded than before, feeling a bit woozy and not quite myself, whenever I went to move my face, it felt all stiff on the right side, so I went looking for the closest mirror, sure that something was the matter, only to find the right side of my face twisted to the left, paralyzed and numb. Now if you know anything about Jamaican culture, you'll know we believe there's a cup of tea for every ailment in the book. While that may be true, knowing what tea to use is just as essential. I wasted 12 hours that day arguing with a bunch of know it all's who insisted that a cup of ginger tea could fix my face, or that I was just having a pregnant moment. Finally Ricky, a close family friend decided at midnight to take me to the hospital. The doctors diagnosed me with Bell's palsy, enlightening me to the fact that it was caused by added stress, and made worse by sleeping directly under the air unit.

The stress factor was obvious, but I couldn't help but travel a few weeks back, when my mother and I got into one of our very heated arguments, prior to my father's arrival. I'd had enough of her throwing it in my face, always picking at the subject like a scab, never allowing the wound to truly heal. I mustered all the courage I could find to shut her up, telling her she was just mad that I was beautiful, that she was just bitter because he didn't even see her and never loved her. Words I didn't mean, but they cut like a knife, returning the pain of the blows she'd been throwing for so many years.

Now my mother's a beautiful, deep, rich black skin woman, but that day, I swear she turned red in the face.

With no ammo left in the tank she looked me in the eyes and swore that when she came from Jamaica and paid a visit to her "Obeah" man, I wouldn't be looking so beautiful anymore. Acknowledging the science, but choosing to believe the old saying, belief kills and it cures, I chose the doctor's theory, which also kept my sanity in check.

The next couple of months were hell for me, it's as if this woman intended for me to go crazy or lose my child. All she did was pick arguments and fights, but I learnt that I could choose silence in the midst of anger, and ignored her. Something deep inside gave me the feeling a great storm was out there brewing, as if a constant dark cloud lingered above my head.

Sure enough a few days before I was due to go into labor my father appeared at the house. She'd pay close attention as to ensure I was in the dark to her plans. Clearer than ever before, I truly saw, understood, accepted that both my parents were truly jacked in the head. One was a suicidal pedophile and the other a narcissist.

Because of the added stress of him being there, the protein levels in my urine rose so high, they raised an alarm due to the Bell's palsy and the high blood pressure that caused it, causing my doctor to order some tests, which involved me collecting urine over a 24 hour period.

January 23rd, 05, was supposed to be a routine drop off of a urine sample. Ms. Grace came to my aid as always, facing the bitter conditions of the road that night, provoked by the blizzard, and worsened by the crowd of people that filled the streets, as the Eagles had won the right to play in the Super Bowl for the first time in over 40 years. Staring out that window as the car crept safely to its destination, the night began feeling magical, with the snow falling, the happy people in the streets, and in that quick moment of bliss, I felt a stirring in my womb, but giving birth for the first time, how could I know that was a sign towards delivery sometime soon?

As they checked the sample, I felt another stirring but this one I didn't need experience to understand. My "bomboclauts" alerted the nurse to the distress I was in, I was hooked up and checked out, only to learn that the next time I walked through those hospital doors, there would be no baby in my belly. I was so thankful to have Ms. Grace and her only baby girl Simone, who I'd just learn was my cousin, on my mother's side. They'd been the ones by my side all those years; they should be there to witness this miracle, with Tash being the only missing piece. Instead my mother bullied her way into giving orders. She even managed to take Tasha off my list of persons, inviting my father in her stead.

She had to be kidding me, she really expected me to open up myself, my nakedness, be at total peace with that man in the room. I couldn't do it! I begged and pleaded for her to have him leave the room, but my requests fell on deaf ears, unaware at the time of my right to have them removed, and needing somewhere to go once the baby was born, she convince me this was his first grandchild, and he should be there. As far as I saw it, he forfeited any and all rights to such titles, when he decided to break the sacred vow of being a parent.

As if my body decided that it wasn't having that shit either, my pelvic refused to dilate, and as if my baby could feel my pain, and my wanting to protect her, she refused to come. I was in labor for just about 24 hours, when finally they decided a C-Section was necessary as my pressure was always a concern.

Naturally she volunteered herself to come into the operating room, as long as it wasn't him, all that mattered beyond that point, was the safety of my baby girl.

As they cut me open, I went into a full on seizure attack, and as it all went black I looked over to see my mom with a tear down her cheek, scared out of my mind, thinking I was going to die then and there, which confused the fuck out of me because she could have prevented it all.

The Preeclampsia I was diagnosed with since my father's arrival, almost took the life of me and my child. The next time I opened my eyes, groggy from all the medicine, I was awakened by a strong loud cry as the medicine wore off, and just knew it was the cries of my baby girl. When the nurses finally bought her to me, I just sat there, rocking her, singing, all snotty nosed, happy to have survived, if only to feel the warmth of her touch.

The first time I held that child, I knew perfect love. No conditions, no reasons, just love in its purest state. She gave me new reason to live, and I decided it was time to get my shit together, grow up, and be a better mother to her than my parents had been to me. She was my lucky charm in some ways, as if the more I loved and cared for this soul, the less space there was for the hate, anger and bitterness. She gave me the power I needed to take back their ability to get me upset at the mere mention of their names.

My father hung around for another week, helping me out, back and forth to doctors, trying his best to show that he was trying to change, but his apologies were always so empty, and never ended without the word, but, so I kept a close eye on him, and never let myself be fooled into being comfortable around him. I'd become weary of my mother also, as she'd proven to me twice that her love and loyalty for him ran deeper than any for me. My aim was to remain as humble as I could for my baby's sake, kissing ass, knowing in due time I'd be sticking my foot up there one day. The worst part of it all, was that after he left, she honestly felt as if she'd done absolutely nothing wrong, behaving as if her actions were perfectly normal. Whenever I asked why she'd put me through that hell, she said he'd change, and deserved a second chance to make things right.

My work permit arrived finally, when my baby was a few months old. The timing couldn't have been more perfect as I was now able to make my own money, which meant independence.

Despite all the horrible things that had happened between us, my mother seemed to have a soft spot for the baby, either that or she was just doing for the glory from others, as they saw her helping me, either way she took the baby to work with her when she could, helping me to save a few dollars to get on my feet and out her house.

She laid the final straw that broke the camel's back in the biggest, loudest brawl we'd ever had. It began like any other fight, ending with her telling me as usual that it was somehow all my doing. This particular day though she felt the need to go a bit too far, telling me that she was sorry he didn't do more to me than he actually had. "Mi sorry him neva cut yuh throat when he was done with you". The next thing I knew, my mouth flung open, and I found myself telling her that it was ok that she wished those thoughts, so long as she remembered that every time she kissed him she was technically tasting me.

Child, everything went upside down and inside out in that room. "You little slut, you tek mi man and come now in front of me to brag about it? I know just how to fix you! When I go Jamaica and pay my "obeah" man fi set you, not even doctor can make you walk again".

Remembering what happened the last time, I used what little I had saved up, and moved on out of that woman's house, not because of fear, but because of the stories I had discovered while digging up news on her past. Learning that she even went as far to as to "tie" her husband for him to never be able to leave her, and if it was all true, who knew how far she'd go to keep that man.

A few weeks of being settled into our new place I found out I'd be going for the interview which would determine whether or not I would become a lawful U.S resident. The old case I caught in my teenage years had to be proven dismissed, which meant I had to fly out to Florida to collect the disposition letter in person. While I was there I decided to go for a stroll with my baby girl along the shores. As we walked I notice my legs starting to feel weak, and then suddenly as the water washed up to my ankles, I began falling. Each time I stood up and attempted to try again, I was knocked down by the next wave. Eventually after a little rest, I managed enough strength to get back to my hotel room. With no more attacks for the rest of the trip, I shrugged it off as a weird phenomenon.

A few weeks after returning home, walking up the stairs of my second story apartment, baby in hand, I fell on the stairs. What made it strange was that I didn't trip; instead my legs just gave out in the thigh muscle. The next thing, my arm did the same, and I quickly realized that all was not well, when it became a just about everyday thing.

The doctors diagnosed it as Myasthenia Gravis, giving up after the many trials and tests to find out what it was not. I took the medication that was prescribed, and followed all the doctor's orders, but if you ever get the time to research what that illness can do, you'd understand when I say that I knew it would be a trying road to recovery, if at all, with all the doctors predicting the worst possible outcome themselves. Hard as I tried to accept their diagnoses, I thought of my mother's words, always wondering if there was any truth to it. The mere fact that you would wish that on your child is beyond me. Whatever the underlying causes, I knew I had to detach myself, to heal myself. There was simply too much toxicity in my life as I'd known it, a new start was beyond scary, but it was more than necessary, as my very life depended on it, and so did my child's.

I relocated to NY once more, bouncing from place to place, sleeping on different friend's couches, and eventually ending up in a homeless shelter. As fate had it that would be one of the best things that ever happened to me, as I ended up in a battered women's shelter, which was much safer and offered a real chance at a second chance, if you really yearned for it.

The words of the teachers that took the time to care were displayed in my daily character, using them to remind myself daily that I lived in the shelter, but by no means bounded by it, I refused to adapt to the shelter system and lifestyle.

This caught the eyes of my social worker, who suggested that I enter for the chance to win a scholarship to St. Johns University. Over ten thousand people entered, and when the forty names were called, my name was a part of the list, my essay was chosen. The best part was to know that it all happened because I had the strength to walk away from ideas I once held as truth.

I began meeting new and beneficial people, who opened my eyes to new thoughts, and new ways of thinking, understanding the true power in my own thoughts. I slowly began to realize, the hate I harbored towards my past, was slowly eating away at my future. To truly heal, I had to come to a place where I truly understood I had done absolutely nothing wrong, where my parents were concerned. That it was ok to forgive myself first, and as jacked up as it all seemed at the time, even my parents. My father had an illness that I couldn't change, the inability to own his wrongs in totality, and keep his hands away from children. My mother with whom I can share some understanding of initial doubts, as I've since grown to see the true depths of my father's manipulative powers, but none-the-less bore the guilt of literally throwing me to the dogs, but still I had to let it all go if had any chance of breaking the cycle, for my baby's sake.

As a human, that's sometimes easier said than done, but the harder I worked at it, the more things improved.

After a few failed attempts, due to faults all my own, I finally became legal in the U.S, August 08'. Again as if cashing in my karma points or that great source from which I came as always was looking out, I was awarded an apartment as a part of my scholarship, with carfare and books as a bonus.

Sitting in the huge window of my bedroom one day, staring out at the sun, watching the traffic of the Van Wyck, pulling on a big ole "spliff", giving thanks for all that I'd survived, for the chance to learn that I was the only obstacle in my way, I decided from that moment to live free, and always to remember the promise I made under that "Ackee" tree.

12

Eventually I ended up in my mother's house once more, and a few more times in between. Somehow something always happened to land me on my face, and my insecurities, and the secret wish I held for so many years, to win her love, kept pulling me back to Philly.

Not long after returning, we got into another one of our blowouts, I asked her for the first time, why it is that she never loved me, or if she did why she stopped?

"I did love you, up until you were about six years old. That's when your father started giving you more attention than he did to me".

My heart was broken for her, and for the first time I asked myself if perhaps she had suffered the same fate in a time before. She'd never hugged me or told me she loved me, even telling me that monkeys were more suitable parents, as they held their young close to them, and she didn't. For what it was worth, at least I now had the answer I had yearned after for many years.

Remembering the words of a wise friend I'd met on my new path, about forgiveness, that it doesn't mean letting them back in, it simply means you let it go, so you can be free, and as Madea had put it to me, it's for you, not them.

 With that I blessed her, forgave her, and moved out, understanding finally it was ok for her to not love me back, as that was a choice, as it was equally ok for me to understand that she had to die, figuratively, for me to truly live. I knew in some way or another, she would feel all that she had rained on me, already certain that she had to have had difficulties sleeping at night.

As karma would have it my father's old habits got him into quite a bit of trouble. Back in 2006, he moved his new woman into the house with her five children, the eldest who happened to be 14 years old, and a girl. Being the unsuspected pedophile he was he couldn't resist the urge to touch a young girl, even writing her letters, professing his love.

Somehow the authorities learnt of his actions, and with the slow changes being made in the police force for the better, they began investigating him.

A few months into the investigation, after dropping the youngest off to school, an argument ensued between the two, she was found dead and him with a bullet to the neck.

As the saying goes, God don't like ugly, he survived, and after healing up enough to withstand prison he was hauled off to await trial. If you've heard anything about the prison system in Jamaica, you could imagine the horrors behind those walls. Perhaps that gave me some satisfaction, that some justice had been served in my favor, after all those years, he would finally know what it felt like to be controlled. But his past employment granted him favors, and he got an easier pass than the other inmates, so in my eye he still never truly was punished.

Staying committed to my vow to truly forgive him, I even went to the prison a few times to see if we could have some sort of friendship. Well I thought that's what forgiving meant, you know, letting it go so much that we could pretend none of it ever happened, and a really big part of me wanted to believe that definition. He seemed to be doing good, became a minister in the prison, even hosting the prison's Christian radio station. But the depth of his manipulative ways were revealed, after I had done some investigating of my own, to see if perhaps that woman had died defending her child.

According to him, the incident occurred once, and was stopped immediately after the child refused his advances. He told me that her aunt was bitter over her sister's death, and was using the incident as ammo. He spoke in that voice he used to all those years ago, and immediately I knew he was lying. That and the fact that he was being investigated prior to the shooting, which meant she knew.

Even after he'd done so much, and after so many knew, they all let it go, aunts of mine, his sisters, past colleagues, he was so powerfully manipulative, he even had me, the victim, ready to wipe his slate clean. He even had me helping in his parole process. It wasn't until the reality hit that in time the prison would release a sick man onto the streets, withheld for some time, but never treated. I thought of all the little Moniques that would be at his disposal once he was free to roam the island, and even more frightening was the fact that he'd now tasted prison and could possibly kill to not go back. I thought of the ones like myself, for who it was too late to prevent the memories already stored, but could be saved if they knew they were not alone.

How many Jennifer's, nosey neighbors, teachers, and family friends there were, in the same predicament? How many mothers are out there, so trapped by a predator's manipulative, destructive ways, so much as to neglect her own child? That promise I made under that "Ackee" tree is the reason you are reading these words right now.

This journey began just over fifteen years ago, when I wrote the first manuscript, stolen from beneath my mattress, and handed over to my mother, and though I was discouraged, I was never deflated. Grateful even that Ms. Grace delayed my path, as now I can bring this work to you from a place of true healing. A place where I am no longer ashamed of a past I survived, no longer afraid of what the whispers will say, but instead, ready to speak out bravely to all the little Moniques out there, to let them know it is not your fault, the only time it becomes that, is when you choose to give up. Grateful that I can now speak to anyone who is seeing but not speaking, to encourage you to say something, your voice may very well save a child, and put an end to a culture that is too sociably accepted, and ignored.

To you who will interact with the person that may be broken, to not be so quick to judge, but to think for a moment that you just never know what lies behind a smile or that slutty behavior.

To the person who thinks that rape happens only when a door is kicked in, please understand, it begins the moment no is uttered, be it verbal or action. To the culture that says if she had only put on some more clothes that wouldn't have happened. For the mentality to shift to an understanding that no one can be claimed as property, with a sole purpose of satisfying any person's sexual desires, or to be held hostage to their ego.

Most of all I wrote this story for any person that's ever had their power taken, to tell you that it can only ever be permanently taken, the moment you decide to give up taking it all back. Understanding that forgiving doesn't mean keeping those persons close, it is truly for you and no one else and in doing so it doesn't make you weak, but strong beyond measure.

The purpose of this book is to show how forgiveness can heal and cure, but as the saying goes some things are easier said than done. How does one summon the strength it really takes to be the person I am today? Statistically I should have killed myself, been prostituted, drugged up somewhere, or spending the rest of my days in a bitter march with placards professing my hatred for all men. So how exactly do you get to a place of forgiving?

I tried so many different outlets, and it would be gravely unfair to give credit to any one person, god, or book, as I adopted many principles of self-healing from them all, but I suppose the greatest lesson was found in the eyes of a 6 year old child.

My daughter came home from school one day with an open palm clearly printed in her face, swollen and red. Irritated at the mere fact that anyone thought they had the right to violate my child, and harboring trust issues with strangers bringing her harm, I began yelling as loudly as my lungs would allow, asking her what happened, demanding to know how she handled it., even threatening that she had better dished the same to them.

My six year old looked me in the eyes, face all bruised up and said, "Mom, if I hit them back, then I'm no better. They need love not more hate, that's why they picked on me."

In that moment I truly learnt what Mr. Mandela meant when he spoke of leaving the pain behind in the jail cell, understanding that was the only true way to be free from imprisonment on the outside. You see truly choosing to let it all go definitely seems unfair, but think about it this way whether you forgive them or not it doesn't undo the action, it keeps you in a place of constantly allowing them to hurt you through pain and anger whenever you remember. You have nothing but the pain and anger to lose anyway by giving forgiveness a chance, nothing else. Why walk around, wanting to die, while they live with joyful memories of the pain they inflicted.

I say put all that pain on the abuser, not the abused.

Let the person who abused you, let them know how much they hurt you. Don't be afraid to confront them. Get in their face about it! Take your power back!!!

Many will try to silence you, tell you to forget, get over it, and just keep quiet. Let no one take your voice away, NO ONE!!!

My most heartfelt letter to you, those without the courage to speak, those who have been shunned, shamed and scorned this goes out to you. You are not alone, take comfort in knowing if we stand together we can prevent, and change the idea and culture of rape for future generations. No more broken children.

I often asked god if you made me in your image and knew me before I was formed, then why make me in an image he would desire so much. What could I have done differently to prevent the abuse? Tape my breast down? Wear more clothes? Hide my physical developments? I did all of that and he still touched me. I found every reason to blame me for what happened, instead of blaming my perpetrator.

Confronting him through text on fb one day, I let him know how despicable and unforgivable his actions were, but that I chose to forgive him, so that I could be free. Not surprising he replied, stating that had both parents been in the household, all this would have been avoided.

I realized then that the only way to keep my word and help someone else, was to put pride aside, speak up and speak out.

Today I am not where I wanted to be, but so much further, and although my journey still requires a lot of growth, I give thanks that I am here now to share my story with you. I am now 30, happy and doing my best to join the change on the education of rape. To convince you to think twice before you assume that child is rude, or she's just a whore. To changing a culture who always says, no matter what she did she is still your mother. To open the eyes of a society who blame the victim so harshly while we neglect to convict the monsters.

It is my hope to especially change the mindset of people in Jamaica, and other small islands, or wherever rape or molestation exists, that it never was and will no longer be acceptable to sweep it under the rug.

Though I am the whole ocean in a drop, I am still but a drop of a larger whole, and through the efforts of this whole my vision is to, if not change the subculture and mindset of rape, to at least spark the mind that will create that change.

Keeping my word true, each book purchased will take me one step closer to creating a safe haven in Jamaica for children and victims of sexual abuse and incest, just as I wished so many years ago for such a place to have existed.

Finally this book was my last milestone in truly becoming a survivor. Fifteen years ago the manuscript was stolen, and my dream delayed, but here we are, with you reading my words.

The words of a true SURVIOR!!!

26333389R00081

Printed in Great Britain
by Amazon